Great Year-Round GRILLING in the WEST

The Flavors • The Culinary Traditions • The Techniques

Ellen Brown

The Lyons Press
Guilford, Connecticut
An Imprint of the Globe Pequot Press

This book is dedicated to David Krimm and Peter Bradley—the two best almost-brothers
a woman could have—who grill wonderful treats on their San Francisco grill.

To buy books in quantity for corporate use
or incentives, call **(800) 962–0973**
or e-mail **premiums@GlobePequot.com.**

The Lyons Press is an imprint of The Globe Pequot Press

Photos on the following pages courtesy of Shutterstock: ix, 3, 8, 9, 10, 12, 16, 17, 21, 25, 26, 29, 31, 36, 48, 51, 55, 64,
65, 67, 79, 90, 92, 95, 96, 97, 99, 110, 111, 115, 116, 117, 119, 121

Photos on the following pages courtesy of Jupiterimages: x, 1, 2, 5, 39, 40, 47, 50, 56, 60, 61, 72, 80, 101, 102, 104, 112,
123

Photo (black and white) on page x courtesy of the Library of Congress

Text design by Sheryl P. Kober

Library of Congress Cataloging-in-Publication Data
Brown, Ellen.
 Great year-round grilling in the West : the flavors--the culinary traditions--the techniques / Ellen Brown.
  p. cm.
 ISBN 978-1-59921-483-2
 1. Barbecue cookery--West (U.S.) 2. Cookery, American--Western style. I. Title.
 TX840.B3B758 2009
 641.7′60978--dc22
                                                                                    2008042720

Printed in China
10 9 8 7 6 5 4 3 2 1

Contents

Chapter 1: **Grilling Fundamentals** 1

This chapter includes everything you need to know about grills and grilling to successfully cook all the recipes in the book, beginning with the principles of grilling; charcoal vs. gas grills; accessories for ease and safety; grilling safety; how to gauge when the grill is ready to cook; how to use wood chips to add smoky flavor to foods; and how to create multi-level fires.

Chapter 2: **Ways to Flavor Food: Rubs, Pastes, Marinades, and Brines** 7

There are four basic ways to flavor food before it goes on the grill—rubs, pastes, marinades, and brines—and the amount of time required to impart flavor ranges from seconds to days. Some encompass cooking from various regions of America, as well as cuisines from around the world.

Chapter 3: **Sauces for Basting and Topping** 15

This chapter includes sauces to dress up grilled food and elevate a simple entree to a dish of distinction. These sauces are versatile, and can go with many types of food; each recipe is annotated with the categories of grilled food for which it is compatible.

Chapter 4: **Hors d'Oeuvres and Appetizers** 21

Grilled hors d'oeuvres are as varied as slices of toasted bruschetta topped with fresh tomatoes to Thai chicken satay with peanut sauce. What differentiates hors d'oeuvres from appetizers is that the former are "finger food" and can be eaten without a plate and fork.

Chapter 5: **Soups and Small Vegetable Salads** 29

Grilling adds its flavor to the main ingredients that go into soups, and in the same way small salads can be topped with grilled fare or include grilled ingredients. The salads in this chapter are small appetizers rather than the larger salads in Chapter 11.

Contents

Contents

Preface

To me, grilling is more than a way of cooking; it's a way of life. The process of grilling food arouses so many sensual pleasures that the end result is more than just a meal. Perhaps that is the reason why I grill year-round; the aroma of food cooking on the grill is as welcome when bundled up against the January cold as it is when lounging in the balmy breezes of July.

Grilling is hardly an exact science; every fire, even one ignited on a gas grill, is different, just as every piece of food cooked on it is unique. The temperature of the air, the velocity and direction of the wind, and the relative humidity all have to be factored into how long it will take a grill to heat and how long it will take food to cook on it. That means that your eyes play a major role when grilling to judge what "done" means, as you poke at food to judge its texture. The sound of food searing adds aural expectation to the experience, and then there's the aroma—emerging not just from the grill but also from the food itself as the steam rises from the plate and reaches the nose.

Grilling, more than any other cooking method, provides an opportunity to share the process with those who will benefit from the results. While a few friends might keep me company in the kitchen from time to time, conventional cooking is basically a solitary endeavor. But a grill becomes the center of a social event, and hovering around it while chatting or sipping is anticipation of a meal that both the cook and the guests can enjoy. Grilling is part of Americans' way of life, be it limited to the summer months in some states and year-round in others.

Most of my personal grilling has taken place in the Northeast. I currently live in Rhode Island, but I grilled on beaches and decks on Nantucket for more than a decade prior to moving here, lit many grills in tiny Georgetown courtyards while living in Washington, and spent childhood summers grilling on the sandy shores of Long Island.

But during the past twenty-five years I have traveled extensively researching American cuisine, both its historic roots and contemporary manifestations. As the founding food editor of *USA Today*, my editorial charge was to transform food journalism—a local "beat" tied to supermarket advertising—to encompass national trends. Much of my time was spent on the Pacific Coast because that was where food was "happening." I chronicled the emergence of New American Cuisine in California, Hawaii, and the Pacific Northwest as I also detailed the culinary histories of these states, as well as those of the Rocky Mountains.

Each state—even regions within a state—has a distinct pattern of cookery determined by the nationalities of the first settlers who joined the Native Americans who had been living on the land for centuries.

But this early culinary history has been tempered by the waves of immigrants who arrived from the nineteenth to twenty-first centuries, and as the size and scope of our larder is increasing exponentially with air travel and modern agricultural practices. That is why there are so many international dishes along with traditional American foods in this book; it is those foods that reflect the America of today and the various ethnic heritages that are now blended into those of the original settlers.

I hope you enjoy grilling the dishes in this book, and I hope that as you grill them you allow the pleasures of grilling to become a larger part of your life.

Ellen Brown
Providence, Rhode Island

While writing a book is a solitary endeavor, its publication is always a team effort. My thanks go to:

Eugene Brissie of The Lyons Press for envisioning such an exciting project.

Ed Claflin, my agent, for his constant support and great humor.

The talented staff at Lyons Press, especially to Ellen Urban for her knowledgeable editorial guidance, Diana Nuhn for the crash course she provided on photo selection, Jessie Shiers for her eagle-eyed editing, and Sheryl Kober for her inspired design.

Constance Brown and Kenn Speiser, my dear neighbors and friends, who good-heartedly ignored the constant smoke from my grills wafting into their backyard from mine.

My many friends whose palates and culinary savvy aided me in recipe development, most especially my beloved sister, Nancy Dubler.

Tigger and Patches, my furry companions, who personally endorse all fish and seafood dishes.

Introduction

The History of Food Traditions in the Pacific and Mountain States

By the time settlers in the early and mid-nineteenth century crossed the grasslands of the Midwest, arrived at the Rocky Mountains, and moved beyond to the shores of the Pacific Ocean, what they brought with them was truly American food. While immigrants from Germany, Scotland, the Scandinavian countries, and many other countries were part of the wagon trains, the majority of settlers were already native-born Americans. Their foods were based on the American regional cookery that had developed along the Atlantic Coast in the seventeenth and early eighteenth centuries and in the Midwest and along the Gulf Coast during the decades that followed the Revolutionary War.

As is true of the development of all American fare, settlers—primarily farmers who were attracted to inexpensive land and miners looking to pan their fortunes by finding gold—had to temper their culinary concepts against what the land would support and what they could assimilate from the Native American tribes that had inhabited the region for centuries. Rather than bringing the yeast-risen breads of Europe, settlers brought the cornbread of Kentucky and Texas; rather than attempting to replicate pies from England, they brought familiar pies from New England.

In the same way that the Spanish introduced foods to the Atlantic colonies via settlements in Florida and along the Gulf Coast, the Spanish also brought

The rich aquatic treasures of the Pacific are masterfully displayed at the famous Pike Place Market in Seattle.

European crops to California via Mexico. Everything from almonds and apricots to peaches and walnuts arrived when the Franciscan priests established missions; the first was in San Diego in 1769. As wheat became more abundant, in 1786 the monks established a flour mill to supplement corn tortillas with those made from flour, in the tradition of Arizona. Food in California remained in the Spanish-Mexican tradition until the Gold Rush of 1849, when more than 80,000 settlers arrived.

Between 1840 and the Civil War, while Californians were searching for gold, the lure of a new frontier with free land in the Oregon territory drew thousands of settlers from as far away as New England and the Carolinas, as well as the recently settled Missouri and Mississippi River valleys.

Two settlers from Iowa, Henderson Luelling and William Meek, were the Pacific Northwest's agricultural trailblazers. They arrived with root stock and started a nursery in the Willamatte Valley, where they planted the ancestors of today's Rogue River pears and Hood River apples.

While it was gold rather than crops that caused a swell in the population of Washington State in 1855, the settlers there found the same fertile valleys and growing conditions as existed in Oregon. Washington is now the leading state in apple production, as well as many other crops.

In these three Pacific Coast states, riches were gathered from the sea as well as from the land. Salmon had sustained Native Americans in the Pacific Northwest since prehistoric times, and those tribes living at the mouth of the Columbia River had perfected the intricate fishing techniques necessary to catch them, as well as oysters and crab.

These same species, along with halibut and trout, are culled from the cold waters off Alaska as well. In the mid-eighteenth century Russian Czar Peter the Great dispatched Captain Vitus Bering to explore the Alaskan coast; it took almost forty years more for a permanent settlement to begin on Kodiak Island. These early Russian influences are still evident in communities like Sitka, where grains such as buckwheat groats are popular.

After Alaska was purchased by the United States in 1867, paddle wheelers began regular journeys up

Hawaii is the only state in which pineapples are grown.

great inland rivers carrying supplies. However, the state remained barely populated until gold was discovered in the Yukon in 1896, when Alaska became the gateway to the Klondike gold fields.

No contrast could be greater than between the frozen tundra of Alaska and the lush Hawaiian islands, but the two share one similarity; until the arrival of the first humans in the third century CE, these isolated areas supported no edible plant life. From other islands in the South Pacific, these first Hawaiians brought some two dozen plants—including the important taro and sweet potato—as well as animals to domesticate as food.

In 1778 Captain James Cook sighted the islands, and they were soon incorporated into all the trade routes across the Pacific, so it was not uncommon for eighteenth century New England families to enjoy fresh pineapple when boats would pull into port. Hawaii is now the country's tropical Garden of Eden, with such crops as pineapples, coconuts, and macadamia nuts emblematic of its riches.

Fishermen catching salmon on the Columbia River in 1919.

During the nineteenth and well into the twentieth century, such cultural rituals as the luau and native Hawaiian cuisine coexisted alongside the dishes of the European settlers: *haole* food. Between the 1880s and 1930s, the third wave of immigrants arrived in the islands, this time primarily Asian immigrants from China, Japan, Okinawa, and Korea, as well as Portuguese from islands in the Atlantic Ocean.

Foods from these cultures became part of the mix we now call Hawaiian cuisine, truly the first great example of Fusion cooking in the country. The Asian prototype dishes remained more pure than those integrated into other regions of American cooking, but they did utilize indigenous crops and aquatic species.

All of the states discussed thus far share the waters of the Pacific; however, the other cluster of states whose foods are included in these recipes share the rugged terrain of the Rocky Mountains—Idaho, Montana, and Wyoming.

It is not by accident that Idaho is now synonymous with the potato, which remains the state's chief crop. The state's rich volcanic soil along with melting snow provide the perfect combination, and botanist Luther Burbank's hybrid, perfected in 1872, became the mainstay of the crop. The rough-skinned Russet Burbank potato is internationally known as the Idaho potato today. Mormons grew the first commercial potatoes in the late nineteenth century.

Idaho's population was expanded by settlers from both the British Isles and Scandinavian countries, and the territory also gained a significant Basque population in the late nineteenth century. Arriving to work both as miners and sheepherders, this pocket of immigrants brought the culinary heritage of the Iberian peninsula, including lusty lamb dishes and chorizo sausage.

A fondness for lamb was also prevalent in Montana, which was settled in the mid-nineteenth century after the discovery of gold and copper in the mountains. For the first century, raising livestock was the territory's primary agricultural function, but that was replaced by growing wheat in the twentieth century.

The European settlement of Wyoming began about the same time as in the other mountain states, and by the beginning of the twentieth century the population had become international, with more than forty nationalities represented.

Until the end of the twentieth century, the Pacific states may have followed culinary trends, but now they set them for the rest of the nation. Some of the most exciting New American Cuisine was spawned in the 1980s along this coast.

First dubbed California Cuisine, chefs in the Bay Area of California encouraged local farmers to raise boutique crops destined for the plates of local diners, with such chefs as Alice Waters and Jeremiah Tower leading the way. While at first the emphasis was on using locally raised and farmed ingredients to cook essentially French country food, the movement then became focused on elevating prototypes from American regional cooking to a new level of sophistication.

Chapter 1

Grilling Fundamentals

The unifying factor to most of the recipes in this book—excluding many desserts and side dishes—is that at some point food comes into contact with a grill. This chapter introduces you to the basic equipment and techniques used when grilling food.

Charcoal Grills

All charcoal grills have two grates; the lower grate holds the charcoal and the upper grate holds the food. Charcoal briquettes or hardwood charcoal rest on the lower grate, and once they are lit you can move them around to create the heat pattern that is best for each recipe.

The temperature of the fire is controlled by opening and closing the top and bottom vents. The more these vents are open, the hotter the fire will be, and the more they are closed, the cooler the fire.

Charcoal briquettes are the fuel used overwhelmingly by charcoal grillers, accounting for almost 90 percent of the charcoal purchased in 2007. Invented by automotive pioneer Henry Ford, briquettes are made of low-quality, powdered charcoal and binders that are compressed and molded into little black pillows.

An alternative to briquettes is hardwood charcoal, created by burning hardwood in a furnace using very little oxygen. A piece of hardwood charcoal is almost pure carbon, and has neither glue nor additives present. While almost double the cost of generic briquettes, it does burn hotter and the fire can be controlled more effectively than using briquettes.

Starting a charcoal fire is hardly difficult, and depending on how many accoutrements you want to buy, you can accomplish the job with very little effort. Here is a summary of the primary ways charcoal fires are lighted:

Unlike conventional cooking, grills can be set up anywhere, including on secluded beaches.

- **Lighter fluid.** This petroleum product is very volatile, and should be used with extreme caution. Arrange charcoal in a pyramid in the center of your grill, and spray the coals evenly with the fluid until saturated. Allow the liquid to penetrate for 1 minute, and then light the coals in locations all around the base of the pyramid with a long match or a long-handled butane lighter. Never use additional lighter fluid once the coals have been initially lit and are smoldering.

One of the great twentieth-century innovations was the covered kettle grill.

- **Self-starting charcoal briquettes.** These are briquettes that are pre-soaked so only lighting is necessary. My suggestion is to start with ten to twelve pre-soaked briquettes, and once they are flaming add conventional charcoal on top. Your food is less likely to develop the petroleum taste associated with lighter fluid.

- **Chimney charcoal lighter.** These are becoming increasingly popular because they do not involve petroleum, but they are a problem to take along for a cookout away from the house because of their bulky size. They are essentially a metal tube with a handle on one side. Inside is a grate to hold the charcoal and a chamber underneath for crumpled newspaper. Light the newspaper using a match or lighter, and set the chimney on the grill grate. The chimney effect takes the newspaper's flames up through the charcoal and lights it. When a white ash forms on the charcoal, pour the lighted coals out onto the charcoal grate.

Tips for All Charcoal Grills

While charcoal grills range from small ones designed for picnics to ones encased in extravagant outdoor kitchens, certain rules apply. The key to success when grilling over charcoal is how well the fire is built, and then how well it is maintained if grilling for a long duration. Here are some of considerations for all charcoal fires:

- **Use enough charcoal.** This is perhaps the most common foible of charcoal grilling, regardless if the food to be grilled is a lowly hotdog or a luxurious tenderloin of beef. Make sure the fire is 4 inches larger in diameter than the food to be cooked over it. The higher the charcoal is banked, the hotter the fire will be. If you want to cook over a very hot fire, build the coals to within 3 inches of the grate on which the food will cook. Determine the amount of charcoal you need by piling it up under the cooking grate, and then push it into a pyramid for easy lighting or place it in a chimney.

Charcoal briquettes are stacked up in a chimney starter, with newspaper stuffed into the bottom chamber for fuel.

- **Make sure the charcoal is ready.** Whether using briquettes or hardwood charcoal, the visual sign is that all pieces are lightly covered with gray ash. This means that the charcoal is fully lit and hot.

- **Clean out the ashes regularly.** The heat of a charcoal fire can be diminished if the bottom vents are clogged with ashes. Remove both grates, close the bottom vents, and scoop out the ashes. Remember to open the vents before lighting the next batch of charcoal.

- **Close down the grill after cooking.** There is no reason to waste charcoal, so close the top and bottom vents on the grill to shut it off. The half-used charcoal can be placed off to the side and used to refresh the next fire.

Gas Grills

There is no question that a gas grill is more convenient than cooking with charcoal. Lighting a gas grill is like lighting the oven broiler, and gas grills offer unparalleled convenience. Many people believe, however, that what is lost is some of the flavor and aroma transferred to food when cooking on a charcoal grill.

Gas grills use natural or LP gas for heat and flames, so the fire is efficient. Here is how to light most of them, although you should always consult the manufacturer's instructions: Open the cover, and then open the valve of the gas tank. One at a time, turn the controls to high and ignite the corresponding burner with either a long butane lighter, a long match, or the burner's own electronic ignition. Close the cover and wait 15 to 20 minutes for your grill to reach its highest heat.

Gas grills are becoming increasingly popular due to the convenience of merely turning on a burner.

Stopping a gas grill is just as easy as lighting one. Turn off each burner, and close off the gas valve. Then turn one of the burners on high for 15 seconds to bleed any gas remaining in the line, turn that burner off, and close the cover.

Tips for All Gas Grills

Gas grills are convenient, but there are also some innate safety problems because you are cooking with a highly volatile liquid. Here are some considerations for safety as well as achieving the best flavor:

- **Always keep the lid down except if expressly told to leave it open in a recipe.** Gas burns cleanly, so no residue accumulates on the interior of the lid from high-heat cooking.

- **Remove the warming rack, assuming the grill has one, before lighting the grill.** Unless you plan to actually use it, the warming rack gets in the way of turning food at the back of the grate, and can burn your hand as you try.

- **Do not skimp on the preheating time.** It is easy to know when a charcoal fire is ready for cooking, and with a gas grill your only clue is how long it has been heating. Give it a full 15 minutes, and longer in cold weather.

- **Store propane tanks—full or empty—in a well-ventilated space.** They should *never* be placed in a garage or basement.

Grilling Accessories

Gourmet shops and web sites are filled with grilling accessories, but there are only a few that are really necessary. Here is a brief list of ones I find useful:

- **Spray bottle.** For problems to be serious enough that a fire extinguisher is necessary is not common; however, minor flare-ups caused by fat dripping onto either charcoal or metal bars are a routine occurrence when grilling. A spray bottle—either purchased for the grill or a well-washed-out one

from a cleaning product—is important to keep around at all times. You can target the flames without disturbing the food above them.

- **Stainless-steel tongs.** You should have a few pairs of tongs, with handles at least 12 inches long. Use tongs and *not* a meat fork for turning food (a meat fork causes food to lose juice and become dry).

- **Spatula.** A long-handled spatula makes flipping hamburgers and moving other foods easy.

- **Grill brush.** Use a grill brush to clean the grate on which the food sits. I clean it once at the end of grilling, and then again before adding food the next time.

- **Instant-read thermometer.** This piece of inexpensive equipment should be mandatory in every kitchen, not only for grilling but for roasting as well. All you have to do is stick it into the thickest part of food and leave it in for 20 seconds, and it registers an accurate reading on the doneness of your food.

- **Metal and bamboo skewers.** While metal skewers are indestructible, they are not as aesthetically pleasing as delicate ones made from bamboo.

Using Wood Chips for Flavor

Wood chips made from aromatic woods like hickory, mesquite, apple, and cherry add immeasurably to the flavor of grilled foods, as well as giving the skin of poultry a rich mahogany color. For charcoal grills, the secret is to soak the chips in water to cover for at least 30 minutes. Even though it is not as pronounced a flavor, you can also use wood chips on a gas grill. Place about 2 cups dry wood chips in the center of a large (12 x 18-inch) piece of heavy-duty aluminum foil. Bring up the foil on all sides and roll the ends together to seal the pouch. Poke several small holes in the top of the packet. Once the grill is hot, place the wood chip pouch under the grate across the burner shields. Smoke will eventually emerge from the holes.

Long handles are the primary requirement for cooking tools used at the grill.

Fire Configurations for Grilling

Each recipe in this book contains information about the appropriate temperature and configuration of the grill for the success of the recipe. This section guides you through what each of these mean.

- **Direct grilling.** This was how all grilling was accomplished prior to the invention of the covered kettle grill and the gas grill. The coals are lit and then evenly spread three to four layers deep on the lower grate.

- **Dual-temperature grilling.** Once the coals are ignited and have reached the desired temperature, you can customize the fire to the needs of the food. By spreading the coals so that they are three or four deep on one side of the grill and one or two layers deep on the other side, you can sear food and then transfer it to the cooler side to complete the cooking. For a gas grill, preheat the grill on high, and then reduce half the burners to medium.

- **Indirect grilling.** When you are cooking by indirect heat on a charcoal grill, what you are actually doing is turning your covered grill into an outdoor oven. The coals are pushed to the periphery of the grill and the food is place in the center over an aluminum drip pan rather than over direct heat. The grill is always kept covered, and the top and bottom vents are partially closed. If you have a gas grill with more than one burner, it is possible to cook over indirect heat. The grills best suited to indirect cooking are those with right and left rather than front and back burners.

Determining the Temperature of a Grill

After the coals have a light coating of ash or the gas burners have been preheated, place your hand, palm-side down, about 4–5 inches above the cooking rack, and count slowly. Here are your readings to determine the temperature of the grill.

- Hot grill: 2 seconds

- Medium-hot grill: 3–4 seconds

- Medium grill: 5–6 seconds

- Medium-low grill: 7 seconds

Grilling is a high-heat cooking method, so if you can hold your hand over the coals for more than 7 seconds, it means you should be adding more coals or preheating the gas burners longer.

Preparing the Grill Grate

Once the grill grate has heated from the fire, take a stiff wire grill brush and brush it well to remove any cooked-on food remaining.

Treating the grid with oil just prior to grilling helps ensure that food will not stick. The best way to do this is to dip a paper towel in vegetable oil, and then, holding it with tongs, rub it all over the grill grate. This is an important step to good grilling.

The Timing of Recipes and How to Use This Book

There is no universal style of cookbook and recipe writing; each author approaches the task in a somewhat personal way. In order to provide you with the maximum number of recipes, the preparation of the fire refers you back to this chapter rather than using space to restate it constantly.

Each recipe is annotated with the number of servings, which is usually given as a range. If the dish is part of a multi-course meal, it can be "stretched" to feed more people; if it is an item that is one-per-person, the number of servings is finite.

"Active time," the second annotation, is the amount of hands-on prep time needed in the kitchen before food goes to the grill. In almost all cases the amount is less than 25 minutes, or less than the amount of time needed for a charcoal grill to heat properly. This is the time measurement for all the chopping, dicing, and indoor cooking.

The third annotation is "Start to finish." While grilling is a cooking method that can be considered "fast food" because it cooks with high heat, the time needed to properly light and heat the grill must always be factored into the equation; it may take only 5 minutes to cook a pounded chicken breast, but that is *after* the grill is ready to accomplish the task.

The recipes in this book are calculated to factor in the fire preparation as part of the time necessary to complete the dish, and to be on the safe side, the assumption is 25–30 minutes.

Chapter 2

Ways to Flavor Food: Rubs, Pastes, Marinades, and Brines

There are basically four ways to flavor food before it goes on the grill—rubs, pastes, marinades, and brines—and the amount of time required to impart flavor ranges from seconds to days. In this chapter you will find recipes and techniques for all these ways to treat food destined for the grill.

Rubs

Rubs are a relatively new addition to the arsenal of ways to flavor foods, and they truly do offer flavor without fuss. Most rubs are highly concentrated mixtures of herbs and spices that should be applied to food after it has been brushed with oil. And "rub" is what you should do. Rather than just giving food a light sprinkle, the mixture should be rubbed into the food with your fingertips, at which time it is ready to grill.

Creole Rub

Yield: ½ cup | Active time: 5 minutes | Start to finish: 5 minutes | Uses: All foods

Combine paprika, garlic powder, onion powder, oregano, thyme, pepper, and cayenne in a bowl, and mix well. Store in an air-tight container in a cool, dry place for up to 1 month.

3 tablespoons paprika
2 tablespoons garlic powder
1 tablespoon onion powder
1 tablespoon dried oregano
1 tablespoon dried thyme
2 teaspoons freshly ground black pepper
1 teaspoon cayenne

South of the Border Rub

Yield: ½ cup | Active time: 5 minutes | Start to finish: 5 minutes | Uses: All foods

Combine chili powder, paprika, cumin, coriander, garlic powder, oregano, black pepper, and red pepper in a bowl, and mix well. Store in an air-tight container in a cool, dry place for up to 1 month.

2 tablespoons chili powder
2 tablespoons paprika
1 tablespoon ground cumin
1 tablespoon ground coriander
1 tablespoon garlic powder
1 tablespoon dried oregano
1 teaspoon freshly ground black pepper
1 teaspoon crushed red pepper flakes

7

3 tablespoons dry mustard

2 tablespoon garlic powder

2 tablespoons coarsely ground black pepper

1 tablespoon dried oregano

2 teaspoons dried basil

Steakhouse-Style Rub

Yield: ½ cup | Active time: 5 minutes | Start to finish: 5 minutes | Uses: Beef, lamb

Combine mustard, garlic powder, pepper, oregano, and basil in a bowl, and mix well. Store in an air-tight container in a cool, dry place for up to 1 month.

2 tablespoons ground coriander

2 tablespoons dried thyme

1 tablespoon ground cumin

1 tablespoon freshly ground black pepper

1 tablespoon dried oregano

1 tablespoon dried sage

Aromatic Herb and Spice Rub

Yield: ½ cup | Active time: 5 minutes | Start to finish: 5 minutes | Uses: All foods

Combine coriander, thyme, cumin, pepper, oregano, and sage in a bowl, and mix well. Store in an air-tight container in a cool, dry place for up to 1 month.

Spices, such as peppercorns and fennel seeds, should be crushed in a mortar and pestle to release their flavor.

Spices are used around the world, and they add vibrant color as well as flavor to foods.

Pastes

Pastes represent the middle ground between rubs and marinades, and the amount of time needed to use them is more than a rub but less than a marinade. Pastes are highly concentrated in the same way as rubs, but they also contain some perishable ingredients for accent flavors, so they are moist. Many pastes have oil added to create the proper thick texture. They should be rubbed onto meat, and allowed to sit for at least 20 minutes, or about the same amount of time it takes for a grill to heat.

Lemon-Herb Paste

Yield: ½ cup | Active time: 10 minutes | Start to finish: 10 minutes | Uses: Chicken, fish and seafood, pork, veal

Combine tarragon, thyme, lemon zest, garlic, and pepper in a bowl, and mix well. Add oil, and mix into a paste. Store in an air-tight container, refrigerated, for up to 3 days.

3 tablespoons dried tarragon

2 tablespoons dried thyme

2 tablespoons grated lemon zest

4 garlic cloves, peeled and pressed through a garlic press

2 teaspoons freshly ground black pepper

3 tablespoons olive oil

Fresh herbs add their aroma and color to pastes and marinades.

1 (2-ounce) tube anchovy paste

6 garlic cloves, peeled and pressed through a garlic press

1 tablespoon Dijon mustard

2 teaspoons herbes de Provence

½ teaspoon freshly ground black pepper

¼ cup extra-virgin olive oil

Provençal Paste

Yield: ½ cup | Active time: 10 minutes | Start to finish: 10 minutes | Uses: Fish and seafood, chicken

Combine anchovy paste, garlic, mustard, herbes de Provence, and pepper in a bowl, and mix well. Add oil, and mix into a paste. Store in an air-tight container, refrigerated, for up to 3 days.

3 tablespoons grated fresh ginger

5 garlic cloves, peeled and pressed through a garlic press

2 tablespoons ground cumin

2 tablespoons turmeric

1 tablespoon ground cardamom

½ teaspoon cayenne

4 tablespoons olive oil

Tandoori Paste

Yield: ½ cup | Active time: 10 minutes | Start to finish: 10 minutes | Uses: Beef, lamb, chicken, fish and seafood

Combine ginger, garlic, cumin, turmeric, cardamom, and cayenne in a bowl, and mix well. Add oil, and mix into a paste. Store in an air-tight container, refrigerated, for up to 3 days.

Marinades

Marinades are a time-honored stalwart of cooking. If given enough time, food will definitely absorb the flavor, and marinades can also render less expensive cuts of meat buttery tender. To tenderize, some sort of acid must be present. Vinegars, with the exception of rice wine and balsamic, are too strong; wines and citrus juices are far more delicate, and the food will have a complex flavor from the combination of ingredients rather than having any one dominate.

The following chart will give you some general guidelines to marinating different types of food. Keep in mind that the thinner the food, the less time is needed to achieve a meaningful flavor. Also, heartier foods require longer than delicate foods.

Marinating Foods: How Much and For How Long		
FOOD	LIQUID PER POUND	TIME
Beef	½ cup	3–24 hours
Lamb	½ cup	3–24 hours
Pork	½ cup	2–12 hours
Veal	½ cup	1–3 hours
Chicken, with skin and bones	⅓ cup	4–12 hours
Chicken breasts, boneless and skinless	⅓ cup	30 minutes–3 hours
Turkey, whole	1 cup	24 hours
Turkey breast cutlets	⅓ cup	30 minutes–3 hours
Duck, whole	½ cup	4–24 hours
Delicately flavored fish fillets (sole, halibut), and shellfish	¼ cup	30 minutes
Strongly flavored fish fillets/steaks (tuna, bluefish)	¼–½ cup	30 minutes–1 hour
Tender vegetables (mushrooms)	¼ cup	1–2 hours
Thick-skinned vegetables (peppers, eggplant)	¼ cup	2–4 hours

6 scallions, rinsed, trimmed, and sliced

3 jalapeño or serrano chiles, seeds and ribs removed, and diced

3 garlic cloves, peeled

½ cup vegetable oil

¼ cup soy sauce

2 tablespoons freshly squeezed lime juice

1 teaspoon ground allspice

2 teaspoons granulated sugar

1½ teaspoons dried thyme

½ teaspoon ground cinnamon

½ teaspoon ground ginger

Freshly ground black pepper to taste

Jamaican Jerk Marinade

Yield: 1 cup | Active time: 15 minutes | Start to finish: 15 minutes | Uses: Pork, chicken

Combine scallions, chiles, garlic, vegetable oil, soy sauce, lime juice, allspice, sugar, thyme, cinnamon, ginger, and pepper in a food processor fitted with a steel blade, or in a blender. Puree until smooth. Transfer mixture to a heavy resealable plastic bag, add food to be marinated, and turn the bag to coat food evenly.

Note: The marinade can be refrigerated for up to 3 days, tightly covered.

¼ cup freshly squeezed lime juice

3 tablespoons tequila

2 tablespoons triple sec

1 large jalapeño or serrano chile, seeds and ribs removed, and finely chopped

2 garlic cloves, peeled and minced

2 teaspoons grated lime zest

1 tablespoon chili powder

1 teaspoon ground cumin

1 teaspoon granulated sugar

Salt and freshly ground black pepper to taste

¼ cup vegetable oil

Margarita Marinade

Yield: ¾ cup | Active time: 10 minutes | Start to finish: 10 minutes | Uses: Chicken, fish and seafood

Combine lime juice, tequila, triple sec, chile, garlic, lime zest, chili powder, cumin, sugar, salt, and pepper in a heavy resealable plastic bag, and mix well. Add oil, and mix well again. Add food to be marinated, turning the bag to coat food evenly. Marinate food according to chart above.

Note: The marinade can be refrigerated for up to 3 days, tightly covered.

To preserve both color and potency, spices should be kept in a cool, dry, dark place.

Hearty Red Wine Marinade

Yield: 1 cup | Active time: 10 minutes | Start to finish: 10 minutes | Uses: Beef, lamb, venison

Combine wine, vinegar, gin, brown sugar, thyme, rosemary, garlic, orange zest, lemon zest, bay leaves, cloves, salt, and pepper in a heavy resealable plastic bag, and mix well. Add oil, and mix well again. Add food to be marinated, turning the bag to coat food evenly. Marinate food according to chart above.

Note: The marinade can be refrigerated for up to 3 days, tightly covered.

½ cup dry red wine

2 tablespoons balsamic vinegar

2 tablespoons gin

2 tablespoons firmly packed dark brown sugar

2 tablespoons chopped fresh thyme or 2 teaspoons dried

2 tablespoons chopped fresh rosemary or 2 teaspoons dried

3 garlic cloves, peeled and minced

2 teaspoons grated orange zest

1 teaspoon grated lemon zest

2 bay leaves, crumbled

¼ teaspoon ground cloves

Salt and freshly ground black pepper to taste

¼ cup olive oil

Beer Marinade

Yield: 1 cup | Active time: 5 minutes | Start to finish: 5 minutes | Uses: Chicken, fish and seafood

Combine beer, lemon juice, Worcestershire sauce, garlic, thyme, salt, and pepper sauce in a heavy resealable plastic bag, and mix well. Add oil, and mix well again. Add food to be marinated, turning the bag to coat food evenly. Marinate food according to chart above.

Note: The marinade can be refrigerated for up to 3 days, tightly covered.

¾ cup lager beer

3 tablespoons freshly squeezed lemon juice

1 tablespoon Worcestershire sauce

3 garlic cloves, peeled and minced

1 tablespoon fresh thyme or 1 teaspoon dried

Salt and hot red pepper sauce to taste

3 tablespoons olive oil

Spicy Asian Orange Marinade

Yield: ¾ cup | Active time: 5 minutes | Start to finish: 5 minutes | Uses: Pork, chicken, fish and seafood

Combine mirin, soy sauce, orange juice concentrate, garlic, chile paste, and orange zest in a heavy resealable plastic bag, and mix well. Add vegetable oil and sesame oil, and mix well again. Add food to be marinated, turning the bag to coat food evenly. Marinate food according to chart above.

Note: The marinade can be refrigerated for up to 3 days, tightly covered.

¼ cup mirin or plum wine*

2 tablespoons soy sauce

2 tablespoons orange juice concentrate, thawed

4 garlic cloves, peeled and minced

1 tablespoon Chinese chile paste with garlic*

2 teaspoons grated orange zest

2 tablespoons vegetable oil

2 tablespoons Asian sesame oil

* Available in the Asian aisle of most supermarkets and in specialty markets.

Brines

Brining, along with smoking and salting, is the way that food was preserved prior to refrigeration and freezing. As is true with marinating, the larger the piece of food, the longer it will take to absorb the flavors. Pork chops need to be soaked for only 8–12 hours, while a whole turkey should be brined for the better part of two days.

Apple Cider Brine

Yield: 2 quarts | Active time: 10 minutes | Start to finish: 15 minutes | Uses: Pork, chicken, turkey

1 cup kosher salt

½ cup granulated sugar

1 (6-ounce) can apple juice concentrate, thawed

2 tablespoons whole cloves

3 whole nutmeg, crushed

4 cinnamon sticks, crushed

7 cups cold water

1. Combine salt, sugar, apple juice concentrate, cloves, nutmeg, cinnamon, and 1 cup water in a large non-reactive saucepan, and stir well. Bring to a boil over medium-high heat, stirring occasionally. Reduce the heat to low and simmer 2 minutes.

2. Add remaining water to the pan, and allow brine to cool. Transfer brine to a large container, and add food to be brined. Cover and refrigerate.

Citrus and Herb Brine

Yield: 2 quarts | Active time: 10 minutes | Start to finish: 15 minutes | Uses: Pork, chicken, turkey

1 cup kosher salt

1 cup firmly packed light brown sugar

2 oranges, sliced

2 lemons, sliced

8 garlic cloves, peeled and sliced

¼ cup chopped fresh parsley

2 tablespoons fresh thyme or 2 teaspoons dried

2 tablespoons black peppercorns

1. Combine salt, brown sugar, oranges, lemons, garlic, parsley, thyme, peppercorns, and 1 cup water in a large non-reactive saucepan, and stir well. Bring to a boil over medium-high heat, stirring occasionally. Reduce the heat to low and simmer 2 minutes.

2. Add remaining water to the pan, and allow brine to cool. Transfer brine to a large container, and add food to be brined. Cover and refrigerate.

Chapter 3

Sauces for Basting and Topping

There are chapters later in this book devoted to specific dishes, many of which have sauces to top the food after it comes off the grill. The recipes in this chapter are for sauces that can be served successfully on a wide variety of foods that are grilled without one of the flavoring methods detailed in Chapter 2. The foods are simple so the sauces makes them special.

Ginger Vinaigrette

Yield: 1½ cups | Active time: 10 minutes | Start to finish: 10 minutes | Uses: Fish and seafood, poultry, vegetables

1. Place sesame seeds in a small dry skillet over medium heat. Toast seeds, stirring constantly, for 2 minutes or until lightly brown. Remove the skillet from the heat, and set aside.

2. Combine sesame seeds, vinegar, lime juice, soy sauce, shallots, garlic, ginger, cilantro, salt, and pepper in a jar with a tight-fitting lid, and shake well. Add vegetable oil and sesame oil, and shake well again.

Note: The dressing can be made up to 3 days in advance and refrigerated, tightly covered. Bring it back to room temperature before using.

2 tablespoons sesame seeds
½ cup rice wine vinegar
¼ cup freshly squeezed lime juice
2 tablespoons soy sauce
3 shallots, peeled and minced
3 garlic cloves, peeled and minced
2 tablespoons grated fresh ginger
1 tablespoon chopped cilantro
Salt and freshly ground black pepper to taste
½ cup vegetable oil
¼ cup Asian sesame oil

Hazelnut Vinaigrette

Yield: 2 cups | Active time: 10 minutes | Start to finish: 20 minutes | Uses: Poultry, fish and seafood, vegetables

1. Preheat the oven to 350°F. Place hazelnuts on a baking sheet and toast them for 8 to 10 minutes or until they are lightly browned. Let cool, then transfer to a food processor fitted with a steel blade. Chop hazelnuts finely, using on-and-off pulsing. Set aside.

2. Combine vinegar, Madeira, mustard, sugar, salt, and pepper in a jar with a tight-fitting lid, and shake well. Add hazelnut oil and hazelnuts, and shake well again.

Note: The dressing can be made up to 3 days in advance and refrigerated, tightly covered. Bring it back to room temperature before using.

1 cup hazelnuts
3 tablespoons sherry vinegar
3 tablespoons Madeira
1 tablespoon Dijon mustard
1 teaspoon granulated sugar
Salt and freshly ground black pepper to taste
1 cup hazelnut oil

My Favorite Barbecue Sauce

1 (20-ounce) bottle ketchup

1 cup cider vinegar

½ cup firmly packed dark brown sugar

5 tablespoons Worcestershire sauce

¼ cup vegetable oil

2 tablespoons dry mustard

2 garlic cloves, peeled and minced

1 tablespoon grated fresh ginger

1 lemon, thinly sliced

½–1 teaspoon hot red pepper sauce, or to taste

My Favorite Barbecue Sauce

Yield: 4 cups | Active time: 10 minutes | Start to finish: 40 minutes | Uses: Meat and poultry

1. Combine ketchup, vinegar, brown sugar, Worcestershire sauce, vegetable oil, mustard, garlic, ginger, lemon, and red pepper sauce in a heavy 2-quart sauce-pan, and bring to a boil over medium heat, stirring occasionally.

2. Reduce the heat to low and simmer sauce, uncovered, for 30 minutes, or until thick, stirring occasionally. Strain sauce, pressing with the back of a spoon to extract as much liquid as possible. Ladle sauce into containers and refrigerate, tightly covered.

Note: The sauce can be made up to 1 week in advance and refrigerated, tightly covered. Bring it back to room temperature before serving.

Basque Tomato Sauce

Yield: 4 cups | Active time: 15 minutes | Start to finish: 45 minutes | Uses: meats, poultry, fish and seafood

1. Heat oil in a saucepan over medium-high heat. Add ham, onion, green pepper, and garlic and cook, stirring frequently, for 3 minutes, or until onion is translucent. Add parsley, thyme, bay leaf, tomatoes, tomato sauce, and sherry, and bring to a boil, stirring occasionally.

2. Reduce the heat to low and simmer sauce, uncovered, for 30 minutes, stirring occasionally. Remove and discard bay leaf, and season sauce to taste with salt and pepper. Serve hot.

Note: The sauce can be made up to 3 days in advance and refrigerated, tightly covered. Reheat it to a simmer over low heat, stirring occasionally.

- 3 tablespoons olive oil
- ¼ pound finely chopped smoked ham
- 1 medium onion, peeled and diced
- 1 green bell pepper, seeds and ribs removed, and diced
- 4 garlic cloves, peeled and minced
- 2 tablespoons chopped fresh parsley
- 1 tablespoon fresh thyme, or 1 teaspoon dried
- 1 bay leaf
- 3 (14.5-ounce) cans diced tomatoes, undrained
- 1 (8-ounce) can tomato sauce
- ½ cup dry sherry
- Salt and freshly ground black pepper to taste

Herbed Tomato Sauce

Yield: 2 cups | Active time: 15 minutes | Start to finish: 1 hour | Uses: Meats, poultry, fish and seafood, vegetables

1. Heat olive oil in 2-quart saucepan over medium heat. Add onion and garlic and cook, stirring frequently, for 3 minutes, or until onion is translucent.

2. Add carrot, celery, tomatoes, parsley, oregano, thyme, and bay leaves. Bring to a boil, reduce heat to low, and simmer sauce, uncovered, stirring occasionally, for 40 minutes, or until lightly thickened. Season to taste with salt and red pepper flakes.

Note: The sauce can be made up to 3 days in advance and refrigerated, tightly covered. Bring back to a simmer before serving. It can also be frozen for up to 3 months.

- ¼ cup olive oil
- 1 medium onion, peeled and finely chopped
- 4 garlic cloves, peeled and minced
- 1 carrot, peeled and finely chopped
- 1 celery rib, rinsed, trimmed, and finely chopped
- 1 (28-ounce) can crushed tomatoes
- 2 tablespoons chopped fresh parsley
- 2 tablespoons chopped fresh oregano or 2 teaspoons dried
- 1 tablespoon fresh thyme or 1 teaspoon dried
- 2 bay leaves
- Salt and crushed red pepper flakes to taste

Herbed Tomato Sauce

¾ cup mayonnaise

½ cup sour cream

2 tablespoons white wine vinegar

⅓ pound blue cheese, crumbled

Salt and freshly ground black pepper to taste

Blue Cheese Sauce

Yield: 1½ cups | Active time: 5 minutes | Start to finish: 5 minutes | Uses: Meats, poultry, fish and seafood, vegetables

Combine mayonnaise, sour cream, and vinegar in a mixing bowl, and whisk until smooth. Stir in blue cheese, and season to taste with salt and pepper. Refrigerate until well chilled.

Note: The sauce can be made up to 3 days in advance and refrigerated, tightly covered.

½ pound mild feta cheese, diced

½ cup sour cream

¼ cup plain whole milk yogurt, preferably Greek

¼ cup extra-virgin olive oil

2 tablespoons freshly squeezed lemon juice

2 garlic cloves, peeled

¼ cup chopped fresh dill or 2 tablespoons dried

Salt and freshly ground black pepper to taste

Greek Feta Sauce

Yield: 1½ cups | Active time: 10 minutes | Start to finish: 10 minutes | Uses: Fish and seafood, poultry, vegetables

Combine feta, sour cream, yogurt, olive oil, lemon juice, and garlic in a food processor fitted with a steel blade or in a blender. Puree until smooth. Scrape mixture into a mixing bowl, and stir in dill. Season to taste with salt and pepper, and refrigerate sauce until ready to use.

Note: The sauce can be made up to 3 days in advance and refrigerated, tightly covered.

1 ripe fresh pineapple

½ cup firmly packed dark brown sugar

1 large jalapeño or serrano chile, stemmed and finely chopped

1 cup water

2 tablespoons chopped fresh cilantro

1 tablespoon freshly squeezed lime juice

Pineapple-Chile Sauce

Yield: 3 cups | Active time: 15 minutes | Start to finish: 45 minutes | Uses: Fish and seafood, poultry, vegetables

1. Remove skin from pineapple; remove any eyes with the tip of a sharp knife. Cut pineapple in quarters and discard core, then roughly dice flesh. Combine pineapple, brown sugar, chile, and water in a saucepan and bring to a boil over medium-high heat, stirring occasionally.

2. Reduce the heat to low and simmer sauce, uncovered, over low heat, stirring occasionally, for 25 minutes. Allow mixture to cool, then puree in a blender or a food processor fitted with a steel blade. Stir in cilantro and lime juice, and refrigerate until served.

Note: The sauce can be prepared up to 3 days in advance and refrigerated, tightly covered.

Instant Asian Barbecue Sauce

Yield: 2 cups | Active time: 10 minutes | Start to finish: 10 minutes | Uses: Poultry, fish and seafood, vegetables

Combine applesauce, hoisin sauce, brown sugar, ketchup, honey, rice vinegar, soy sauce, and chile paste in a mixing bowl. Whisk until smooth. Refrigerate until ready to use.

Note: The sauce can be made up to 3 days in advance and refrigerated, tightly covered.

¾ cup unsweetened applesauce

½ cup hoisin sauce*

¼ cup firmly packed dark brown sugar

6 tablespoons ketchup

2 tablespoons honey

2 tablespoons rice vinegar

1 tablespoon soy sauce

1 tablespoon Chinese chile paste with garlic*, or to taste (or hot red pepper sauce can be substituted)

* Available in the Asian aisle of most supermarkets and in specialty markets.

Spicy Thai Peanut Sauce

Yield: 2 cups | Active time: 10 minutes | Start to finish: 30 minutes, including 20 minutes for chilling | Uses: Meats, poultry, fish and seafood, vegetables

Combine peanut butter, water, brown sugar, lime juice, soy sauce, sesame oil, and chile paste in a mixing bowl. Whisk until well combined. Stir in garlic, scallions, and cilantro, and chill well before serving.

Note: The sauce can be made up to 3 days in advance and refrigerated, tightly covered.

1 cup chunky peanut butter

½ cup very hot tap water

½ cup firmly packed dark brown sugar

⅓ cup freshly squeezed lime juice

¼ cup soy sauce

2 tablespoons Asian sesame oil

2 tablespoons Chinese chile paste with garlic*

6 garlic cloves, peeled and minced

3 scallions, rinsed, trimmed, and chopped

¼ cup chopped fresh cilantro

* Available in the Asian aisle of most supermarkets and in specialty markets.

½ medium cucumber, peeled, seeded, and finely chopped

2 ripe plum tomatoes, rinsed, cored, seeded, and finely chopped

2 scallions, rinsed, trimmed, and finely chopped

2 garlic cloves, peeled and minced

1 cup plain whole-milk yogurt

2 tablespoons chopped fresh dill or 2 teaspoons dried

2 tablespoons freshly squeezed lemon juice

Salt and freshly ground black pepper to taste

Dilled Cucumber Raita

Yield: 2 cups | Active time: 10 minutes | Start to finish: 10 minutes | Uses: Meats, poultry, fish and seafood

Combine cucumber, tomatoes, scallions, garlic, yogurt, dill, and lemon juice in a mixing bowl. Stir well, and season to taste with salt and pepper. Refrigerate until ready to use.

Note: The sauce can be made up to 3 days in advance and refrigerated, tightly covered.

---

2 tablespoons olive oil

½ small red onion, peeled and finely chopped

2 garlic cloves, peeled and minced

2 tablespoons ground cumin

3 (4-ounce) cans chopped mild green chiles, drained

1 cup chicken stock or vegetable stock

1 tablespoon cold water

2 teaspoons cornstarch

3 tablespoons chopped fresh cilantro

Salt and freshly ground black pepper to taste

Quick Green Chile Sauce

Yield: 2 cups | Active time: 10 minutes | Start to finish: 25 minutes | Uses: Meats, poultry, fish and seafood, vegetables

1. Heat olive oil in a 2-quart heavy saucepan over medium heat. Add onion and garlic and cook, stirring frequently, for 3 minutes, or until onion is translucent. Reduce the heat to low, stir in cumin, and cook, stirring constantly, for 1 minute.

2. Stir in chiles and stock. Whisk well, bring to a boil, and simmer, uncovered, for 15 minutes, stirring occasionally, or until reduced by one-fourth. Combine cold water and cornstarch in a small bowl, and stir to dissolve cornstarch. Add to sauce, and bring to a simmer, stirring constantly. Cook over low heat for 1–2 minutes, or until sauce has thickened.

3. Stir in cilantro, and season to taste with salt and pepper. Serve hot or at room temperature.

Note: The sauce can be made up to 3 days in advance and refrigerated, tightly covered. Bring it back to room temperature or to a simmer before serving.

Chapter 4

Hors d'Oeuvres and Appetizers

When you have the grill lit for the main course of a meal, it only makes sense to utilize this versatile cooking tool for more than one dish. In this chapter you will find recipes for small nibbles to enjoy with a cocktail or glass of wine before dinner, as well as small first courses—most of them seafood—to serve at table. Many of the recipes in this chapter are excellent for buffet entertaining and cocktail parties too. In addition to the dishes in this chapter, also take a look at the soups and salads in Chapter 5 for other light options to begin a meal.

Barbequed Oysters

2 dozen oysters

⅓ cup bottled chili sauce

2 tablespoons soy sauce

1 tablespoon freshly squeezed lemon juice

1 tablespoon chopped fresh cilantro

Freshly ground black pepper to taste

Barbecued Oysters

Yield: 4–6 servings | Active time: 15 minutes | Start to finish: 40 minutes

1. Prepare a medium-hot grill according to the instructions given in Chapter 1. Scrub oysters well under cold running water. Discard any that do not shut tightly while being scrubbed.

2. Combine chili sauce, soy sauce, lemon juice, cilantro, and pepper in a small bowl. Stir well, and set aside.

3. Place oysters on the grill with rounded side down. Grill, covered, 3–4 minutes. Remove oysters with tongs and place on a hot pad. Remove and discard top shell with an oyster knife, being careful not to spill oyster liquor. Separate oysters from bottom shell, but do not remove oyster.

4. Top each oyster with 2 teaspoons sauce. Return oysters to the grill, and grill, covered, for 2–3 minutes more, or until edges of oysters curl. Serve immediately.

VARIATION: *Large littleneck clams can be substituted for the oysters.*

Note: The sauce can be prepared up to 3 days in advance and refrigerated, tightly covered with plastic wrap.

5 tablespoons unsalted butter

¾ cup finely chopped onion

4 garlic cloves, peeled and minced

1 red bell pepper, seeds and ribs removed, finely chopped

1 ½ cups Italian breadcrumbs

¼ cup freshly grated Parmesan cheese

24 littleneck clams

Clams Casino

Yield: 4–6 servings | Active time: 20 minutes | Start to finish: 35 minutes

1. Prepare a medium-hot grill according to the instructions given in Chapter 1.

2. Melt butter in a large skillet over medium heat. Add onion and garlic, and cook, stirring frequently, for 3 minutes, or until onion is translucent. Add red bell pepper and cook, stirring frequently, for 5–7 minutes, or until peppers are soft. Add breadcrumbs and cheese to mixture and stir to combine. Set aside.

3. Scrub clams well under cold running water. Discard any that do not shut tightly while being scrubbed. Place clams in a mixing bowl, and cover with very hot tap water. Within about 2 minutes shells will be slightly open. Insert a clam knife or paring knife between shells at one corner, and sever the muscles holding the shells together.

4. Mound topping on clams, using about 1 tablespoon per clam. Grill for 5–8 minutes, covered, depending on the size of the clam, or until the clams are hot. Serve immediately.

Note: The topping can be made up to 2 days in advance and refrigerated in a container or heavy plastic bag.

North Beach Marinated Shrimp

Yield: 4–6 servings | Active time: 20 minutes | Start to finish: 40 minutes

1. Soak bamboo skewers in warm water to cover, and prepare a medium-hot grill according to the instructions given in Chapter 1.

2. Place shrimp in a heavy resealable plastic bag, and add ¼ cup olive oil, 2 garlic cloves, 2 tablespoons oregano, salt, and pepper. Mix well, and marinate shrimp at room temperature for 20 minutes, turning the bag occasionally.

3. Combine celery, gardiniera vegetables, pepperoncini, pimientos, remaining garlic, and parsley in a food processor fitted with a steel blade, and chop finely using on-and-off pulsing. Scrape mixture into a mixing bowl.

4. Combine vinegar, lemon juice, remaining oregano, salt, and pepper in a jar with a tight-fitting lid, and shake well. Add remaining olive oil, and shake well again. Add dressing to the bowl with vegetables, and set aside.

5. Remove shrimp from marinade, and discard marinade. Divide shrimp into 4–6 groups, and thread each group onto two parallel skewers. Grill shrimp, covered, for 2 minutes per side, or until pink and cooked through. Remove shrimp from skewers.

6. To serve, place 1 portion lettuce on each plate and top with vegetables and shrimp.

Note: The vegetables and marinade can be prepared up to 1 day in advance and kept tightly covered in the refrigerator.

- 8–12 (8-inch) bamboo skewers
- 1½ pounds extra large (16–20 per pound) raw shrimp, peeled and deveined
- ¾ cup olive oil, divided
- 6 garlic cloves, peeled and minced, divided
- ¼ cup chopped fresh oregano, divided
- Salt and freshly ground black pepper to taste
- ¾ cup diced celery
- ¾ cup chopped pickled Italian gardiniera vegetables
- 12 pepperoncini, stems removed, and chopped
- 4 whole canned pimientos or roasted and skinned red bell peppers
- ½ cup firmly packed fresh parsley leaves
- ½ cup white wine vinegar
- 2 tablespoons freshly squeezed lemon juice
- 4–6 cups salad greens, or 6 large leaves Boston lettuce

2 pounds large sea scallops, rinsed and patted dry with paper towels

¼ cup olive oil, divided

Salt and freshly ground black pepper to taste

1 navel orange

¼ cup freshly squeezed lime juice

½ English cucumber, cut into ⅓-inch dice

¼ small red onion, peeled and chopped

1 small jalapeño or serrano chile, seeds and ribs removed, and finely chopped

¼ cup chopped fresh cilantro

3–4 cups mixed salad greens, rinsed and dried

Marinated Sea Scallops

Yield: 6–8 servings | Active time: 30 minutes | Start to finish: 2 hours, including 45 minutes for marinating

1. Prepare a hot grill according to the instructions given in Chapter 1.

2. Toss scallops with 2 tablespoons oil, and season to taste with salt and pepper. Cut peel (including all white pith) from orange using a small serrated knife. Dice orange, and set aside.

3. Grill scallops, uncovered if using a charcoal grill, turning once, until just cooked through, about 5 minutes. Remove scallops from the grill, and allow to cool. Cut scallops into quarters.

4. Combine scallops, orange, lime juice, cucumber, onion, chile, and remaining oil in a mixing bowl. Season to taste with salt and pepper, and refrigerate scallops, covered, for at least 45 minutes, or until cold.

5. Stir cilantro into scallop mixture. To serve, divide salad greens onto individual plates, and mound scallop mixture in the center.

VARIATION: *Large shrimp, or 1-inch cubes of any firm-fleshed white fish such as cod or halibut can be used in place of scallops.*

Note: The scallops can be cooked and the other mixture can be prepared up to 1 day in advance and refrigerated separately, tightly covered. Do not mix scallops into vegetable mixture more than 2 hours in advance.

Tomato and Olive Bruschetta

Tomato and Olive Bruschetta
Yield: 24 pieces | Active time: 20 minutes | Start to finish: 50 minutes

1. Prepare a medium-hot grill according to the instructions given in Chapter 1.

2. Brush onion with olive oil. Grill onion, turning with tongs occasionally, for 12–15 minutes, or until onion is tender. Remove vegetables from the grill, and allow them to cool.

3. While onion grills, brush bread slices with oil, and grill for 2 minutes per side, or until toasted. Cut 1 garlic clove in half, and rub on 1 side of toast. Set aside.

4. Discarding root end, chop onion. Mince remaining 2 garlic cloves. Combine onion, garlic, tomatoes, feta, olives, chiles, paprika, cumin, and remaining olive oil in a mixing bowl. Season to taste with salt and pepper.

5. To serve, mound topping on toast slices, and serve immediately.

Note: The topping and the toast slices can be prepared up to 3 hours in advance and kept at room temperature.

1 small red onion, peeled and halved lengthwise

¼ cup olive oil, divided

24 slices sourdough baguette, ½ inch thick

3 garlic cloves, peeled

5 ripe plum tomatoes, cored, seeded, and finely chopped

¼ cup crumbled feta cheese

¼ cup chopped black olives

2 tablespoons chopped mild green chiles, drained

1 teaspoon smoked Spanish paprika

½ teaspoon ground cumin

Salt and freshly ground black pepper to taste

4 large poblano peppers

24 slices sourdough baguette, ½-inch thick

¼ cup extra-virgin olive oil

3 garlic cloves, peeled

3 tablespoons chopped fresh oregano or 1 tablespoon dried

1 tablespoon freshly squeezed lemon juice

Salt and freshly ground black pepper to taste

Poblano Chile Sourdough Bruschetta

Yield: 24 pieces | Active time: 20 minutes | Start to finish: 50 minutes

1. Prepare a medium-hot grill according to the instructions given in Chapter 1.

2. Grill peppers on all sides until skin is charred and black, turning them gently with tongs. Remove peppers from the grill, and place them in a heavy plastic bag; allow them to stand for 10 minutes.

3. While peppers are grilling, brush bread slices with oil, and grill for 2 minutes per side, or until toasted. Cut 1 garlic clove in half, and rub on 1 side of toast. Set aside.

4. Remove skin and seeds from peppers, and chop peppers finely. Mince 2 remaining garlic cloves. Combine peppers, garlic, oregano, lemon juice, and remaining olive oil in a mixing bowl. Season to taste with salt and pepper.

5. To serve, mound topping on toast slices, and serve immediately.

Note: The topping and the toast slices can be prepared up to 3 hours in advance and kept at room temperature.

Chicken Satay

Chicken Satay

Yield: 36 pieces | Active time: 15 minutes | Start to finish: 3¼ hours, including 3 hours for marinating

1. Trim fat from chicken breasts and pull off tenderloins. Remove tendon from the center of each tenderloin by holding down tip with your finger and scraping away meat with the dull side of paring knife. Cut tenderloins in half, and cut the remaining chicken meat into 1-inch cubes.

2. Combine soy sauce, brown sugar, lime juice, chile paste, garlic, and sesame oil in a heavy resealable plastic bag, and blend well. Add chicken pieces and marinate, refrigerated, for 3 hours, turning the bag occasionally.

3. Prepare a medium-hot grill according to the instructions given in Chapter 1.

4. Remove chicken from marinade, and discard marinade. Grill chicken pieces, uncovered if using a charcoal grill, turning pieces with tongs, for a total of 3–5 minutes or until brown and cooked through. Spear each piece of chicken with a toothpick or bamboo skewer and serve hot with a cup of Spicy Thai Peanut Sauce for dipping.

VARIATION: *Cubes of pork or beef, large shrimp, or strips of salmon can become satay as well as chicken.*

Note: The chicken can marinate for up to 6 hours, and it can be cooked 1 day in advance and refrigerated, tightly covered. Reheat it in a 350°F oven wrapped in aluminum foil for 5 to 10 minutes, or until hot.

---

4 boneless and skinless chicken breast halves

½ cup soy sauce

½ cup firmly packed dark brown sugar

¼ cup freshly squeezed lime juice

2 tablespoons Chinese chile paste with garlic*

4 garlic cloves, peeled and minced

1 tablespoon Asian sesame oil*

1 cup Spicy Thai Peanut Sauce (recipe on page 19)

* Available in the Asian aisle of most supermarkets and in specialty markets.

1 cup mesquite chips

4 ears fresh corn, unshucked

¾ pound bulk pork sausage

½ cup finely chopped red bell pepper

½ cup finely chopped green bell pepper

3 scallions, white parts and 2 inches of the green tops, trimmed and finely chopped

3 tablespoons olive oil

2 tablespoons freshly squeezed lime juice

2 tablespoons pure maple syrup

Salt and freshly ground black pepper to taste

3 tablespoons finely chopped cilantro

6–8 leaves romaine, rinsed and dried

Grilled Corn and Sausage Salad

Yield: 6–8 servings | Active time: 15 minutes | Start to finish: 1 hour

1. Prepare a medium-hot grill according to the instructions given in Chapter 1. If using a charcoal grill, soak mesquite chips in water for 30 minutes. If using a gas grill, create a packet for wood chips as described in Chapter 1.

2. Remove all but 1 layer of husks from corn and pull out the corn silks. Soak corn in cold water to cover for 10 minutes. Place wood chips on the grill. Grill corn, covered, for 10–15 minutes, turning with tongs occasionally.

3. When cool enough to handle, discard husks, and cut kernels off cobs using a sharp serrated knife.

4. Cook sausage in a frying pan over medium heat, breaking up lumps with a fork. Cook until brown. Combine sausage and its fat with corn, red and green bell peppers, and scallions in a mixing bowl.

5. Combine olive oil, lime juice, maple syrup, salt, and pepper in a jar with a tight-fitting lid. Shake well, and toss with the corn mixture. Toss with cilantro, and serve at room temperature on top of lettuce leaves.

Note: The salad can be made up to 2 days in advance and refrigerated, tightly covered with plastic wrap. Allow it to sit at room temperature for a few hours to take the chill off. Do not add the cilantro until just before serving.

Chapter 5

Soups and Small Vegetable Salads

Hot soups to warm you in winter or chilly soups to cool you in summer are always a welcome way to begin a meal, or a satisfying focus of a light supper or lunch. Most of the recipes in this chapter include component parts that spend some time cooking on the grill, so their aroma and flavor permeates the broth.

Small vegetable salads are another starter as versatile as they are delicious (for grilled salad entrees, see Chapter 11). All of the salad recipes in this chapter can become part of a buffet dinner.

Smoked Garlic Soup

1 cup apple wood or mesquite chips

4 large heads garlic

2 tablespoons olive oil

2 tablespoons unsalted butter

1 large onion, peeled and diced

1 tablespoon fresh thyme or 1 teaspoon dried

5 cups chicken stock

¾ cup heavy cream

Salt and freshly ground black pepper to taste

½ cup freshly grated Parmesan cheese

Smoked Garlic Soup

Yield: 4–6 servings | Active time: 20 minutes | Start to finish: 1 ½ hours

1. Prepare a medium grill according to the instructions given in Chapter 1. If using a charcoal grill, soak apple wood or mesquite chips in water for 30 minutes. If using a gas grill, create a packet for wood chips as described in Chapter 1.

2. Cut top ½ inch off garlic heads and rub oil all over heads, including cut surfaces. Cut 4 (6-inch) squares of heavy-duty aluminum foil, and wrap one around each garlic, allowing the top cut surface to show.

3. Place wood chips on the grill. Grill garlic, covered, for 25 minutes, or until cloves are soft when pressed with the tip of a paring knife. Remove garlic from the grill, and when cool enough to handle, pop cloves out of husks and set aside.

4. Melt butter in heavy 2-quart saucepan over medium-high heat. Add onion and thyme, and cook, stirring frequently, for 3 minutes, or until onion is translucent. Add garlic, stock, and cream, and bring to a boil over medium-high heat.

5. Reduce the heat to low and simmer soup, uncovered, for 15 minutes, stirring occasionally. Puree soup in a food processor fitted with a steel blade or in a blender; this may have to be done in batches. Season soup to taste with salt and pepper.

6. To serve, divide grated cheese among soup bowls and ladle soup over cheese. Serve immediately.

Note: The soup can be made up to 2 days in advance and refrigerated, tightly covered. Reheat soup slowly, but do not let it boil or reduce.

Farmer's Market Vegetable Soup

Yield: 4–6 servings | Active time: 20 minutes | Start to finish: 1 hour

1. Prepare a medium-hot grill according to the instructions given in Chapter 1.

2. Brush eggplant, zucchini, yellow squash, onion, and bell pepper slices with olive oil, reserving 1 tablespoon. Sprinkle vegetables with salt and pepper.

3. Grill vegetables, covered, for a total of 8 minutes, turning them once. Remove vegetables from the grill. Peel pepper, and then cut all vegetables into a ½-inch dice.

4. Heat remaining oil in a heavy 2-quart saucepan over medium-high heat. Add garlic, and cook, stirring constantly, for 1 minute. Add stock, tomatoes, parsley, oregano, and diced vegetables, and bring to a boil. Reduce the heat to low, and simmer soup, uncovered, for 15 minutes, stirring occasionally. Serve immediately.

Note: The soup can be made up to 2 days in advance and refrigerated, tightly covered. Reheat soup slowly, but do not let it boil or reduce.

1 Japanese eggplant, trimmed and cut lengthwise into ½-inch slices

1 zucchini, trimmed and cut lengthwise into ½-inch slices

1 yellow squash, trimmed and cut lengthwise into ½-inch slices

1 medium sweet onion such as Vidalia or Bermuda, peeled and cut into ½-inch slices

1 large red bell pepper, seeds and ribs removed, and cut lengthwise into quarters

¼ cup olive oil, divided

Salt and freshly ground black pepper to taste

2 garlic cloves, peeled and minced

4 cups chicken stock

1 (14.5-ounce) can diced tomatoes, drained

¼ cup chopped fresh parsley

2 tablespoons chopped fresh oregano or 2 teaspoons dried

Farmer's Market Vegetable Soup

1 cup mesquite chips

4 large garlic cloves, unpeeled

8–10 medium ears fresh corn, unshucked

2 tablespoons unsalted butter

¼ cup yellow cornmeal

1 (4-ounce) can chopped mild green chiles, drained

2 cups chicken stock

2 cups whole milk

Salt and freshly ground black pepper to taste

Grilled Corn Soup

Yield: 6–8 servings | Active time: 20 minutes | Start to finish: 1 hour

1. Prepare a medium-hot grill according to the instructions given in Chapter 1. If using a charcoal grill, soak mesquite chips in water for 30 minutes. If using a gas grill, create a packet for wood chips as described in Chapter 1.

2. Preheat the oven to 350°F. Bake garlic cloves for 15 minutes, and peel garlic when cool enough to handle. Set aside.

3. Remove all but 1 layer of husks from the corn, and pull out corn silks. Soak corn in cold water to cover for 10 minutes. Place mesquite chips on the grill. Grill corn, covered, for 10–15 minutes, turning with tongs occasionally. Remove corn from the grill, and when cool enough to handle, cut kernels from cobs using a sharp serrated knife.

4. Melt butter in a large saucepan, and cook kernels over low heat for 5 minutes, stirring occasionally. Remove 1 cup of kernels, and set aside. Puree remaining corn, roasted garlic, cornmeal, chiles, and stock in a food processor fitted with a steel blade or in a blender. This will probably have to be done in a few batches.

5. Combine puree with milk and heat to a boil over medium heat. Add reserved corn kernels, and season to taste with salt and pepper. Reduce the heat to low, and simmer for 5 minutes, stirring occasionally.

Note: The soup can be made up to 2 days in advance and refrigerated, tightly covered. Reheat soup slowly, but do not let it boil or reduce. After it has been chilled, it may have to be thinned with a little additional milk or stock.

2 ripe avocados, peeled and diced

¼ medium onion, peeled and diced

1 garlic clove, peeled

1 (4-ounce) can diced mild green chiles, drained

1 small jalapeño or serrano chile, seeds and ribs removed

Juice of 1 lime

2 cups chicken stock, preferably homemade

½ cup sour cream

½ cup half-and-half

3 tablespoons fresh chopped cilantro

Salt and cayenne to taste

Chopped tomato and crushed tortilla chips

Chilled Avocado Soup

Yield: 4–6 servings | Active time: 15 minutes | Start to finish: 1 hour, including 45 minutes for chilling

1. Combine avocados, onion, garlic, chiles, fresh chile, lime juice, chicken stock, sour cream, half-and-half, cilantro, salt, and cayenne in a food processor fitted with a steel blade or in a blender. Puree until smooth, and chill for at least 45 minutes.

2. To serve, sprinkle individual portions with chopped tomato and crushed tortilla chips.

Note: The soup can be made up to 1 day in advance and refrigerated, with plastic wrap pressed directly into the surface.

Panzanella Salad

Yield: 4–6 servings | Active time: 20 minutes | Start to finish: 1 hour

1. Prepare a medium-hot grill according to the instructions given in Chapter 1.

2. Combine vinegar, orange juice, 2 garlic cloves, orange zest, salt, and pepper in a jar with a tight-fitting lid, and shake well. Add ½ cup olive oil, and shake well again. Set aside.

3. Place tomatoes in a large salad bowl, and sprinkle liberally with salt and pepper.

4. Brush pepper slices, zucchini, and onion with remaining olive oil. Rub bread slices with remaining garlic. Grill peppers and onion, covered, for a total of 4 minutes, and bread slices and zucchini for a total of 3 minutes, turning slices frequently, or until tender. Remove food from the grill.

5. Cut bread and vegetables into 1-inch pieces, and add to bowl with tomatoes. Toss with dressing, and allow to stand for 15 minutes. Serve immediately, sprinkled with parsley.

Note: The dressing can be prepared up to a day in advance and refrigerated; return to room temperature. Bread and vegetables can be grilled up to 4 hours in advance. Do not combine salad ingredients until 15 minutes before serving.

⅓ cup red wine vinegar

¼ cup freshly squeezed orange juice

3 garlic cloves, peeled and minced, divided

2 teaspoons grated orange zest

Salt and freshly ground black pepper to taste

⅔ cup olive oil, divided

1 pound ripe tomatoes, rinsed, cored, and cut into ¾-inch dice

2 red orange or yellow bell peppers, seeds and ribs removed, and cut into 1-inch strips

1 pound zucchini, rinsed, trimmed, and cut on the diagonal into ⅓-inch slices

1 medium red onion, peeled and cut into ¼-inch slices

1 (12-ounce) loaf of hearty Italian bread, cut into 1-inch slices

¼ cup chopped fresh Italian parsley

½ cup kosher salt

2 quarts cold water

2 (1-pound) eggplants, cut into ¾-inch-thick rounds

2 medium zucchini, quartered lengthwise

2 red bell peppers, seeds and ribs removed, and cut into 2-inch strips

1 large sweet onion, such as Vidalia or Bermuda, peeled and cut into ½-inch slices

½ pound large mushrooms, wiped clean with a damp paper towel, trimmed, and halved

⅓ cup olive oil

4 garlic cloves, peeled and minced

3 tablespoons herbes de Provence

Salt and freshly ground black pepper to taste

¼ cup balsamic vinegar

1 cup crumbled feta cheese

½ cup pitted oil-cured black olives, preferably Provençal

¼ cup slivered fresh basil

Provençal Vegetable Salad with Feta

Yield: 4–6 servings | Active time: 20 minutes | Start to finish: 1 hour

1. Combine salt and water in a large mixing bowl, and submerge eggplant slices; use a plate to press them down into the salted water. Soak eggplant for 30 minutes, then drain slices and squeeze to extract as much water as possible.

2. While eggplant soaks, prepare a medium-hot grill according to the instructions given in Chapter 1.

3. Place eggplant, zucchini, red bell pepper, onion, and mushrooms on baking sheet, keeping vegetables segregated. Drizzle with oil and sprinkle with garlic, herbes de Provence, salt, and pepper. Turn vegetables to coat evenly.

4. Begin by placing onion and red bell pepper on the grill, and 4 minutes later add eggplant, zucchini, and mushrooms. Grill vegetables, covered, until tender and lightly brown, turning slices frequently. Vegetables should cook for a total of 10 minutes.

5. To serve, divide vegetables on individual plates or arrange on a platter. Sprinkle with vinegar, feta, olives, and basil. Serve hot or at room temperature.

Note: The vegetables can be grilled up to 4 hours in advance and kept at room temperature.

⅓ cup olive oil

2 garlic cloves, peeled and minced

2 Japanese eggplants, trimmed and quartered lengthwise

1 zucchini, trimmed and quartered lengthwise

1 yellow squash, trimmed and quartered lengthwise

1 small sweet onion, such as Vidalia or Bermuda, peeled and quartered

Salt and freshly ground black pepper to taste

¼ cup balsamic vinegar

½ cup chopped fresh oregano

Mixed Vegetable Salad with Oregano

Yield: 4–6 servings | Active time: 20 minutes | Start to finish: 45 minutes

1. Prepare a medium-hot grill according to the instructions given in Chapter 1.

2. Mix olive oil and garlic. Brush oil on both sides of eggplants, zucchini, yellow squash, and onion.

3. Grill vegetables, covered, for a total of 10 minutes, turning occasionally, or until crisp-tender. Remove vegetables from the grill with tongs, and, when cool enough to handle, cut vegetables into 1-inch slices.

4. To serve, divide vegetables on individual plates or arrange on a platter. Season to taste with salt and pepper, then drizzle with vinegar and sprinkle with oregano.

Note: The vegetables can be grilled up to 4 hours in advance and kept at room temperature.

Chapter 6

Fish and Seafood

While shops only selling fish and seafood are disappearing from the scene, it is worth the effort to search your neighborhood for the best source you can find for fresh fish. Look for a market that offers a varied selection, that keeps its fish on foil placed on top of chipped ice, and that has a level of personal service that allows you to special-order specific varieties or cuts of fish.

Salmon with Hazelnut Butter

Yield: 4–6 servings | Active time: 25 minutes | Start to finish: 40 minutes

1. Prepare a medium-hot grill according to the instructions given in Chapter 1.

2. Rinse salmon, and pat dry with paper towels. Rub salmon with olive oil, sprinkle with salt and pepper, and set aside.

3. Combine hazelnuts, parsley, thyme, rosemary, butter, and lemon juice in a food processor fitted with a steel blade, and chop finely using on-and-off pulsing. Place wine and shallots in a small saucepan and reduce by half. Add half-and-half and reduce by half again. Slowly whisk in hazelnut mixture, and season to taste with salt and pepper.

4. Cook fish, covered, for 4–5 minutes per side, turning gently with a wide spatula, or until fish is opaque at the edges and slightly translucent in the center. Serve immediately, topped with butter sauce.

Note: The butter sauce can be made up to 4 hours in advance and kept hot in a warmed insulated bottle.

Ingredients:

- 4–6 (6–8-ounce) salmon fillets
- 2 tablespoons olive oil
- Salt and freshly ground black pepper to taste
- ¾ cup skinned hazelnuts, toasted in a 350°F oven for 5 minutes
- 4 sprigs fresh parsley
- 2 tablespoons fresh thyme or 2 teaspoons dried
- 2 tablespoons chopped fresh rosemary, or 2 teaspoons dried
- ¼ pound (1 stick) unsalted butter, softened
- 2 tablespoons freshly squeezed lemon juice
- 1⅓ cups dry white wine
- 4 shallots, peeled and finely chopped
- ⅓ cup half-and-half

4 untreated cedar shingles, about 5½ x 10 inches

2 tablespoons vegetable oil

4 (6–8-ounce) salmon fillets, unskinned

½ cup honey

¼ cup freshly squeezed lemon juice

¼ cup grated fresh ginger

2 garlic cloves, peeled and minced

¼ teaspoon ground cinnamon

Salt and freshly ground black pepper to taste

Cedar-Planked Columbia River Salmon

Yield: 4 servings | Active time: 15 minutes | Start to finish: 40 minutes

1. Prepare a hot grill according to the instructions given in Chapter 1. Soak shingles in water to cover for 15 minutes. Remove shingles from water, and rub both sides with oil.

2. Rinse salmon and pat dry with paper towels. Set aside. Combine honey, lemon juice, ginger, garlic, cinnamon, salt, and pepper in a small saucepan, and stir well. Bring to a boil over medium-high heat, and boil until mixture is reduced by half, stirring frequently. Remove the pan from the heat, and set aside.

3. Arrange salmon on oiled planks, skin side down. Brush salmon with glaze, and cook, covered, for 10 minutes, basting with glaze again after 5 minutes. Salmon is cooked when it flakes easily and is slightly translucent in the center. Remove planks from the grill with tongs and a spatula, and serve salmon immediately.

Note: The glaze can be prepared up to 2 days in advance and refrigerated, tightly covered. Reheat over low heat before cooking salmon.

Cedar-Planked Columbia River Salmon

Tuna in Zinfandel Sauce with Beef Marrow

Yield: 4–6 servings | Active time: 15 minutes | Start to finish: 35 minutes

1. Prepare a hot grill according to the instructions given in Chapter 1.

2. Rinse tuna and pat dry with paper towels. Brush tuna with oil, and sprinkle with salt and pepper. Place tuna in the freezer on a baking sheet lined with plastic wrap while the grill heats.

3. Combine wine, shallots, thyme, rosemary, parsley, carrots, celery leaves, and garlic in a nonreactive saucepan, and bring to a boil over high heat, stirring occasionally. Reduce the heat to medium, and simmer until wine is reduced by two-thirds. Strain mixture, pressing with the back of a spoon to extract as much liquid as possible, and return mixture to the saucepan. Whisk in butter, and set aside.

4. While sauce reduces, bring a skillet of salted water to a boil over high heat. Reduce the heat to low, and poach marrow for 45 seconds. Remove marrow from the pan with a slotted spatula, and keep warm.

5. Grill tuna for 2–3 minutes per side for rare tuna, uncovered if using a charcoal grill, or to desired doneness. Serve immediately, topped with a few tablespoons of sauce and 3 slices of beef marrow.

Note: The sauce and marrow can be prepared up to 1 day in advance and refrigerated, tightly covered. Reheat the sauce in a small saucepan, and reheat the marrow in the reheated sauce.

4–6 (8–10-ounce) tuna steaks, 1 inch thick

2 tablespoons olive oil

Salt and freshly ground black pepper to taste

1 bottle full-bodied California Zinfandel

3 shallots, peeled and minced

5 sprigs fresh thyme

1 sprig fresh rosemary

½ bunch fresh parsley

3 carrots, scrubbed and chopped

½ cup celery leaves

2 garlic cloves, peeled

3 tablespoons unsalted butter

12–18 (½-inch-thick) slices beef marrow

Trout with Lemon Butter Sauce

Yield: 4–6 servings | Active time: 25 minutes | Start to finish: 40 minutes

1. Prepare a medium-hot grill according to the instructions given in Chapter 1.

2. Rinse trout and pat dry with paper towels. Rub fish with oil, and sprinkle with salt and pepper. Cut lemon in half lengthwise, and slice 4–6 slices from one half. Tuck slices inside of trout. Squeeze juice from remaining portions of lemon, and set aside.

3. Melt butter in a skillet over medium-high heat. Add bread cubes and cook, turning frequently, until cubes are browned. Remove cubes from the skillet with a slotted spatula, and set aside. Add lemon juice, parsley, and capers to butter, and heat well. Season to taste with salt and pepper, and keep warm.

4. Grill trout for 4 minutes per side, uncovered if using a charcoal grill, or until skin is crisp and flesh is no longer translucent. To serve, top each trout with butter sauce and sprinkle with croutons. Serve immediately.

Note: The butter sauce can be made up to 6 hours in advance and kept at room temperature.

4–6 (12-ounce) rainbow trout, scaled and gutted, with heads left on

3 tablespoons olive oil

Salt and freshly ground black pepper to taste

1 lemon

¼ pound (1 stick) unsalted butter

4–6 slices white sandwich bread, crusts trimmed and cut into ½-inch cubes

3 tablespoons chopped fresh parsley

1 tablespoon small capers, drained and rinsed

4–6 (6–8-ounce) mahi-mahi fillets, about 1 inch thick

¼ cup olive oil, divided

Salt and freshly ground black pepper to taste

2 tablespoons Aromatic Herb and Spice Rub (recipe on page 8)

1 small avocado

3 tablespoons freshly squeezed lime juice

¼ ripe fresh pineapple, core and rind discarded

6 scallions, rinsed, trimmed, and chopped

¼ cup chopped fresh cilantro

Mahi-mahi with Avocado Pineapple Relish

Yield: 4–6 servings | Active time: 20 minutes | Start to finish: 35 minutes

1. Prepare a medium-hot grill according to the instructions given in Chapter 1.

2. Rinse fish under cold running water, and pat dry with paper towels. Rub fillets with 2 tablespoons olive oil, sprinkle with salt and pepper, and rub with Aromatic Herb and Spice Rub. Set aside.

3. Peel avocado, and dice into ⅓-inch pieces. Place avocado in a mixing bowl, and toss with lime juice to prevent discoloration. Dice pineapple into ⅓-inch pieces, and add to avocado, along with scallions and cilantro. Toss gently with remaining 2 tablespoons olive oil, and season to taste with salt and pepper. Set relish aside.

4. Grill fish for 3–4 minutes per side, uncovered if using a charcoal grill, or until almost cooked through and just translucent in the very center. Serve immediately, garnished with relish.

Note: The relish can be prepared up to 4 hours in advance and kept at room temperature, tightly covered.

4–6 (6–8-ounce) thick grouper fillets

⅓ cup olive oil, divided

Salt and freshly ground black pepper to taste

2 tablespoons smoked Spanish paprika

1 tablespoon ground cumin

2 ripe mangoes, peeled and finely chopped

1 medium tomato, rinsed, cored, seeded, and finely chopped

½ yellow bell pepper, seeds and ribs removed, and finely chopped

½ cucumber, peeled, seeded, and finely chopped

½ small red onion, peeled and finely chopped

1 small jalapeño or serrano chile, seeds and ribs removed, and finely chopped

1 garlic clove, peeled and minced

3 tablespoons chopped fresh cilantro

3 tablespoons freshly squeezed lime juice

Halibut with Tropical Fruit Salsa

Yield: 4–6 servings | Active time: 25 minutes | Start to finish: 1½ hours, including 1 hour for salsa to blend

1. Prepare a medium-hot grill according to the instructions given in Chapter 1.

2. Rinse grouper and pat dry with paper towels. Rub fillets with 2 tablespoons olive oil, and sprinkle with salt and pepper. Combine paprika and cumin in a small bowl, and rub mixture on both sides of fillets.

3. Combine mangoes, tomato, bell pepper, cucumber, onion, chile, garlic, cilantro, lime juice, and remaining olive oil in a mixing bowl, and mix well. Season to taste with salt and pepper, and set salsa aside at room temperature for 1 hour for the flavors to blend.

3. Grill fish, uncovered if using a charcoal grill, for 3–5 minutes per side, or until cooked through and just slightly translucent in the center. Serve immediately, each piece topped with salsa.

Note: The salsa can be prepared up to 6 hours in advance and refrigerated, tightly covered. Allow it to reach room temperature before serving.

Teriyaki Halibut

Yield: 4–6 servings | Active time: 15 minutes | Start to finish: 1 hour, including 30 minutes for marinating

4–6 (8–10-ounce) halibut fillets, 1 inch thick

½ cup soy sauce

2 garlic cloves, peeled and minced

2 scallions, white part only, trimmed and finely chopped

2 tablespoons firmly packed light brown sugar

1 tablespoon grated fresh ginger

1 tablespoon freshly squeezed lime juice

2 tablespoons Asian sesame oil

2 tablespoons vegetable oil

Freshly ground black pepper to taste

1. Rinse fish and pat dry with paper towels. Combine soy sauce, garlic, scallions, sugar, ginger, lime juice, sesame oil, vegetable oil, and pepper in a heavy resealable plastic bag, and mix well. Add fish, and marinate at room temperature for 30–40 minutes, turning the bag occasionally.

2. Prepare a medium-hot grill according to the instructions given in Chapter 1.

3. Remove fish from marinade, and discard marinade. Grill fish for 3–4 minutes per side, uncovered if using a charcoal grill, or until almost cooked through and just translucent in the very center. Serve immediately.

VARIATION: *Boneless, skinless chicken breasts, pounded to an even thickness of ½ inch, are as delicious as fish with this marinade. Grill the chicken until it is cooked through and no longer pink.*

Teriyaki Halibut

4–6 (6–8-ounce) swordfish steaks

Salt and freshly ground black pepper to taste

½ pound bacon, cut into small pieces

1 medium onion, peeled and chopped

1 garlic clove, peeled and minced

1 cup chicken stock, divided

1 cup heavy cream

2 teaspoons cornstarch

1½ cups grated smoked cheddar cheese

1 medium tomato, peeled, seeded, and finely chopped

Swordfish with Smoked Cheddar Sauce

Yield: 4–6 servings | Active time: 20 minutes | Start to finish: 40 minutes

1. Prepare a dual-temperature hot-and-medium grill according to the instructions given in Chapter 1. Rinse fish and pat dry with paper towels. Sprinkle fish with salt and pepper, and set aside.

2. Cook bacon in a skillet over medium-high heat until brown. Remove bacon from the pan with a slotted spoon, and discard all but 2 tablespoons of bacon fat. Add onion and garlic, and cook over medium heat, stirring frequently, for 3–5 minutes, or until onion is translucent. Add ¾ cup stock and cream. Bring to a boil, and simmer for 5 minutes. Mix cornstarch with reserved stock, stir well, and add to sauce. Stir sauce over low heat until thickened and bubbly. Add cheese, and stir until melted. Add tomato and reserved bacon, and keep sauce warm.

3. Sear fish for 2–3 minutes per side on the hot side of the grill, uncovered if using a charcoal grill, then transfer fish to the cooler side of the grill and cook for an additional 2–3 minutes per side, or until slightly translucent in the center. Serve immediately, topped with sauce.

Note: The sauce can be prepared up to 2 days in advance and refrigerated, tightly covered. Reheat it in a saucepan over low heat, stirring frequently.

Swordfish with Smoked Cheddar Sauce

Sea Scallops with Mango Salsa and Chili Vinaigrette

Serves: 6–8 servings | Active time: 25 minutes | Start to finish: 40 minutes

1. Soak bamboo skewers in warm water to cover, and prepare a medium-hot grill according to the instructions given in Chapter 1. Rinse scallops and pat dry with paper towels.

2. Combine mango, cucumber, onion, cilantro, 1 tablespoon olive oil, and lime juice in a glass or stainless-steel mixing bowl. Stir gently, and season to taste with salt and pepper. Allow salsa to sit at room temperature for at least 15 minutes to blend flavors.

3. Combine red pepper and vinegar in a food processor fitted with a steel blade or in a blender. With the motor running, slowly add remaining olive oil and chile oil through the feed tube with the motor running to emulsify dressing. Season to taste with salt and pepper, and set aside.

4. Thread scallops onto 2 parallel skewers, sprinkle with salt and pepper, and brush with vinaigrette. Grill skewers, covered, for 1½–2 minutes per side. To serve, drizzle vinaigrette over skewers and place salsa next to them on the plate.

VARIATION: *Extra-large (16–20 per pound) shrimp or cubes of firm-fleshed white fish like cod or swordfish can be substituted for the scallops.*

Note: Both the salsa and the dressing can be made up to 1 day in advance and refrigerated, tightly covered. Allow both to reach room temperature before serving.

Ingredients

- 12–16 (8-inch) bamboo skewers
- 2 pound sea scallops
- 1 large, ripe mango, peeled, seeded, and cut into ¼-inch dice
- ½ small cucumber, peeled, seeded, and finely chopped
- ¼ small red onion, peeled and finely chopped
- 3 tablespoons chopped fresh cilantro
- ¾ cup olive oil, divided
- 2 tablespoons freshly squeezed lime juice
- Salt and freshly ground black pepper to taste
- 1 roasted red bell pepper, seeds and ribs removed, and diced
- ⅓ cup cider vinegar
- ¼–½ teaspoon Chinese chile oil, or to taste

2 pound jumbo shrimp (less than 10 per pound), unpeeled

2 shallots, peeled and chopped

2 garlic cloves, peeled and minced

Juice of 1 lime

½ cup freshly squeezed orange juice

½ cup white wine

2 tablespoons dark rum

2 tablespoons soy sauce

2 tablespoons chopped fresh parsley

1 tablespoon chopped fresh rosemary or 1 teaspoon dried

Salt and freshly ground black pepper to taste

Tropical Shrimp

Yield: 4–6 servings | Active time: 15 minutes | Start to finish: 2½ hours, including 2 hours for marinating

1. Using sharp scissors, cut along middle of the back of shrimp; leave tail and first segment intact. Devein shrimp using a sharp paring knife, but do not remove shells. Rinse shrimp and pat dry with paper towels.

2. Combine shallots, garlic, lime juice, orange juice, wine, rum, soy sauce, parsley, rosemary, salt, and pepper in a heavy resealable plastic bag, and mix well. Add shrimp and marinate, refrigerated, for a minimum of 2 hours or up to 4 hours, turning the bag occasionally.

3. Prepare a medium-hot grill according to the instructions given in Chapter 1. Remove shrimp from marinade, reserving marinade. Grill shrimp, covered, for 3–4 minutes per side, or until cooked through and opaque in the center.

4. While shrimp are grilling, boil down marinade until it is reduced by half. Spoon a few tablespoons over each portion of shrimp. Serve immediately or at room temperature.

VARIATION: *Any firm-fleshed white fish fillet, such as halibut, whitefish, or snapper, can be substituted for the shrimp.*

Chapter 7

Poultry

Famed nineteenth-century French gastronome Jean Anthelme Brillat-Savarin once wrote that "poultry is for the cook what canvas is for the painter." Its inherently mild flavor takes to myriad methods of seasoning, and it is relatively quick to cook, too.

Almost every permutation of chicken is now available in most supermarkets—from whole birds of various sizes to delicate breast tenderloins. However, there are times and reasons why knowing how to do some chicken cutting is advantageous, so here is a brief guide:

- **Pounding chicken breasts:** Some recipes will tell you to pound the breast to an even thickness so it will cook evenly and quickly. To do so, place the breast between 2 sheets of plastic wrap , and pound with the smooth side of a meat mallet or the bottom of a small, heavy skillet or saucepan.

- **Butterflying a whole chicken:** Butterflying is a process of partially boning a whole chicken so that it can be pressed down flat on the grill and will cook over direct heat, and therefore, in less time than if you kept it whole. Turn the chicken with the breast side down, and using poultry shears cut away the backbone from the tail to the head end on both sides, and discard the backbone (or save it for making stock). Open the bird by pulling the halves apart. Use a sharp paring knife to lightly score the top of the breast bone, then run your thumbs along and under the breast bone, and pull it out. Spread the bird flat. Next turn the chicken over. Cut off the wing tips, and you are ready to grill.

4–6 (6-ounce) boneless, skinless chicken breast halves

2 tablespoons vegetable oil

3 scallions, white parts only, rinsed, trimmed, and chopped

3 garlic cloves, peeled and minced

½ cup canned sweetened cream of coconut (not coconut milk)

½ cup freshly squeezed lime juice

2 tablespoons chopped fresh cilantro

2 tablespoons curry powder or to taste

Salt and cayenne to taste

Chicken with Curried Coconut Sauce

Yield: 4–6 servings | Active time: 20 minutes | Start to finish: 1 hour, including 30 minutes for marinating

1. Trim chicken breasts of all visible fat, and pound to an even thickness of ½ inch between 2 sheets of plastic wrap. Place chicken in a heavy resealable plastic bag, and set aside.

2. Heat oil in a small skillet over medium-high heat. Add scallions and garlic and cook, stirring frequently, for 3 minutes, or until scallions are translucent. Scrape mixture into a mixing bowl, and whisk in cream of coconut, lime juice, cilantro, curry powder, salt, and cayenne. Pour half of mixture into the bag, and mix well to coat chicken. Marinate chicken at room temperature for 30 minutes, turning the bag occasionally.

3. Prepare a hot grill according to the instructions given in Chapter 1. Remove chicken from marinade, and discard marinade.

4. Grill chicken for 2–3 minutes per side, uncovered, or until chicken is cooked through and no longer pink. Serve immediately, passing extra sauce separately.

Note: The marinade/sauce can be prepared up to 2 days in advance and refrigerated, tightly covered.

Grilled Chicken Hash

Yield: 6–8 servings | Active time: 25 minutes | Start to finish: 1 hour

1. Prepare a hot grill according to the instructions given in Chapter 1.

2. Trim chicken breasts of all visible fat, and pound to an even thickness of ½ inch between 2 sheets of plastic wrap. Place 3 tablespoons of the olive oil in a mixing bowl, and add garlic, herbes de Provence, salt, and pepper. Mix well. Add chicken breasts and stir to coat them with mixture.

3. Grill chicken for 2–3 minutes per side, uncovered, or until chicken is cooked through and no longer pink. Cut into ½-inch dice, and set aside.

4. Heat butter and remaining olive oil in a large skillet over low heat. Add onions, toss to coat with oil, and cover the pan. Cook over low heat for 10 minutes, stirring occasionally. Uncover the pan, raise the heat to medium, sprinkle with salt, and stir in sugar. Cook for 20 to 30 minutes, stirring frequently, until onions are medium brown. If onions stick to the pan, stir to incorporate the browned juices into the onions.

5. While onions cook, place potatoes in a saucepan and cover with cold water. Salt water and bring potatoes to a boil over high heat. Boil for 12 to 15 minutes, or until very tender when tested with a knife. Drain potatoes and mash them roughly with a potato masher. Add chicken and onions to potatoes and mix well. Season to taste with salt and pepper.

6. Preheat the oven to 450°F. Spread hash into a greased 9 x 13-inch baking pan and bake for 15 minutes, or until the top is lightly brown. Serve immediately.

Note: The hash can be prepared 2 days in advance and refrigerated, tightly covered. Reheat it, covered with aluminum foil, for 10 minutes, then remove the foil and bake for an additional 15 minutes.

4 (6-ounce) boneless, skinless chicken breast halves

⅓ cup olive oil

3 garlic cloves, peeled and minced

1 tablespoon herbes de Provence

Salt and freshly ground black pepper to taste

4 tablespoons (½ stick) unsalted butter

2 large sweet onions, such as Vidalia or Bermuda, peeled and diced

1 teaspoon granulated sugar

1½ pounds small redskin potatoes, scrubbed and quartered

4–6 (6-ounce) boneless, skinless chicken breast halves

1 cup finely chopped fresh cilantro

⅓ cup freshly squeezed lime juice

2 garlic cloves, peeled and minced

1 tablespoon ground cumin

1 tablespoon chili powder

Salt and freshly ground black pepper to taste

⅔ cup olive oil

2 bell peppers of any color, seeds and ribs removed, and quartered

12--16 scallions, white parts and 4 inches of green tops, rinsed and trimmed

8–12 (8-inch) flour tortillas

Salsa, guacamole, sour cream, jalapeños (optional)

Chicken and Vegetable Fajitas

Yield: 4–6 servings | Active time: 25 minutes | Start to finish: 45 minutes, including 30 minutes for marinating

1. Prepare a hot grill according to the instructions given in Chapter 1.

2. Trim chicken breasts of all visible fat, and pound to an even thickness of ½ inch between 2 sheets of plastic wrap. Combine cilantro, lime juice, garlic, cumin, chili powder, salt, and pepper in a heavy resealable plastic bag; mix well. Add olive oil, and mix well again. Pour off half of mixture, and set aside. Add chicken breasts to remaining marinade, and turn well to coat food evenly. Marinate chicken for 30 minutes at room temperature, turning the bag occasionally.

3. While chicken marinates, grill peppers and scallions for a total of 10–12 minutes or until tender, turning once. Remove vegetables from the grill, and when cool enough to handle, cut into thin strips.

4. Remove chicken from marinade, and discard marinade. Grill chicken for 2–3 minutes per side, uncovered, or until chicken is cooked through and no longer pink.

5. Grill tortillas for 1 minute per side, or until grill marks show. To serve, cut chicken crosswise into thin strips, and add to vegetable mixture. Drizzle mixture with some of remaining marinade. One tortilla at a time, place a portion of mixture on the bottom edge of tortilla. Fold over one side, and roll tortilla firmly but gently to enclose filling. Serve immediately, passing salsa, guacamole, or sour cream separately, if using.

VARIATION: *For beef fajitas, substitute flank steak or skirt steak for the chicken. Marinate the beef for 2 to 3 hours, refrigerated. Consult a similar recipe to determine the cooking time.*

Note: Marinade can be made up to 2 days in advance and refrigerated, tightly covered.

Chicken and Vegetable Fajitas

4–6 (6-ounce) boneless, skinless chicken breast halves

¾ cup plain yogurt

2 tablespoons freshly squeezed lemon juice

3 garlic cloves, peeled and pressed through a garlic press

1 tablespoon grated fresh ginger

1 tablespoon ground turmeric

2 teaspoons ground coriander

1 teaspoon ground cumin

Salt and cayenne to taste

2 tablespoons vegetable oil

Tandoori Chicken Breasts

Yield: 4–6 servings | Active time: 15 minutes | Start to finish: 40 minutes, including 30 minutes for marinating

1. Prepare a hot grill according to the instructions given in Chapter 1.

2. Trim chicken breasts of all visible fat, and pound to an even thickness of ½ inch between 2 sheets of plastic wrap. Combine yogurt, lemon juice, garlic, ginger, turmeric, coriander, cumin, salt, and cayenne in a heavy resealable plastic bag. Add chicken, and marinate at room temperature for 30 minutes, turning the bag occasionally.

3. Remove chicken from marinade, and discard marinade. Pat chicken dry with paper towels, and rub with vegetable oil. Grill chicken for 2–3 minutes per side, uncovered, or until chicken is cooked through and no longer pink. Serve immediately.

Note: The marinade can be prepared up to 1 day in advance and refrigerated, tightly covered.

Tandoori Chicken Breasts

Greek Chicken Paillards with Kalamata Relish

Yield: 4–6 servings | Active time: 20 minutes | Start to finish: 35 minutes

1. Prepare a hot grill according to the instructions given in Chapter 1.

2. Trim chicken breasts of all visible fat, and pound to an even thickness of ½ inch between 2 sheets of plastic wrap. Combine lemon juice, garlic, oregano, salt, and pepper in a heavy resealable plastic bag, and mix well. Add 3 tablespoons of olive oil, and mix well again. Add chicken, and marinate at room temperature for 20 minutes, turning the bag occasionally.

3. While chicken marinates, prepare relish. Combine tomatoes, olives, remaining olive oil, and vinegar in a bowl. Season to taste with salt and pepper, and mix well. Add feta, and mix gently. Set aside.

4. Remove chicken from marinade, and discard marinade. Grill chicken for 2–3 minutes per side, uncovered, or until chicken is cooked through and no longer pink. Serve immediately, topping each chicken breast with some of the relish.

Note: The relish can be prepared up to 4 hours in advance and refrigerated, tightly covered.

4–6 (6-ounce) boneless, skinless chicken breast halves

3 tablespoons freshly squeezed lemon juice

2 garlic cloves, peeled and minced

1 tablespoon dried oregano

Salt and freshly ground black pepper to taste

⅓ cup extra-virgin olive oil, divided

1 pint cherry tomatoes, rinsed, stemmed, and chopped

½ cup pitted kalamata olives, chopped

2 tablespoons white wine vinegar

¾ cup crumbled feta cheese

Middle Eastern Chicken

Yield: 4–6 servings | Active time: 10 minutes | Start to finish: 4¾ hours, including 4 hours for marinating

1. Rinse chicken and pat dry with paper towels. Combine vinegar, onion, garlic, parsley, cumin, coriander, sugar, cinnamon, cayenne, and salt in a heavy resealable plastic bag. Mix well, add olive oil, and mix well again. Add chicken and marinate, refrigerated, for a minimum of 4 hours, turning the bag occasionally.

2. Prepare a medium-hot grill according to the instructions given in Chapter 1.

3. Remove chicken from marinade, and discard marinade. Grill chicken, covered, for 12 minutes per side or until white meat registers 160°F and dark meat registers 180°F on an instant-read thermometer. Serve immediately.

VARIATION: *Pork chops can be substituted for the chicken pieces. Consult a similar recipe to determine the cooking time.*

4–6 chicken pieces (breasts, thighs, legs) with bones and skin

¼ cup balsamic vinegar

1 small onion, peeled and chopped

3 garlic cloves, peeled and minced

¼ cup chopped fresh parsley

3 tablespoons ground cumin

2 tablespoons ground coriander

1 tablespoon granulated sugar

1 teaspoon ground cinnamon

½ teaspoon cayenne or to taste

Salt to taste

¾ cup olive oil

Butterflied Lemon-Herb Chicken

2 (3-pound) whole chickens

1 stick (¼ pound) unsalted butter, softened

3 tablespoons chopped fresh parsley

2 tablespoons chopped fresh rosemary or 2 teaspoons dried

1 tablespoon fresh thyme or 1 teaspoon dried

1 tablespoon grated lemon zest

Salt and freshly ground black pepper to taste

½ lemon, seeded and very thinly sliced

4 bricks wrapped in heavy-duty aluminum foil

Butterflied Lemon-Herb Chicken

Yield: 4–6 servings | Active time: 20 minutes | Start to finish: 50 minutes

1. Rinse chickens and pat dry with paper towels. Butterfly chickens according to the instructions given above.

2. Prepare a medium-hot grill according to the instructions given in Chapter 1.

3. Combine butter, parsley, rosemary, thyme, lemon zest, salt, and pepper in a mixing bowl, and mix well. Stuff mixture under the skin of each chicken, being careful not to tear the skin. Lay lemon slices on top of herbed butter.

3. Place chickens over a medium fire skin-side down. Place 2 bricks on top of each chicken. Grill chicken, covered, for 10 minutes. Remove bricks, and turn chickens over. Replace bricks, and cook for an additional 12 minutes or until an instant-read thermometer registers 180°F when inserted into the thigh. Allow chickens to rest for 5 minutes, then cut into serving pieces, and serve immediately.

Note: Rather than using a whole chicken, you can make this dish with the individual parts of your choice. Consult a similar recipe to determine the cooking time.

Asian Duck Breast

Yield: 4 servings | Active time: 20 minutes | Start to finish: 8½ hours, including 8 hours for marinating

1. Rinse duck breasts and pat dry with paper towels. Trim off all extra skin that is not covering meat, and score the remaining skin with a paring knife in a small diamond pattern, being careful not to cut into the flesh beneath the skin. Combine hoisin sauce, mirin, chile paste, cilantro, scallions, garlic, ginger, salt, and pepper in a heavy resealable plastic bag, and mix well. Add duck breasts, and mix well again to coat all surfaces. Marinate duck, refrigerated, for a minimum of 8 hours or overnight, turning the bag occasionally.

2. Prepare a medium-hot grill according to the instructions given in Chapter 1.

3. Grill duck breasts skin side down, uncovered if using a charcoal grill, for 5 minutes, or until skin is browned. Turn duck gently with tongs, and grill other side for 4–6 minutes. Remove duck from grill, and allow it to rest for 5 minutes, lightly covered with aluminum foil. Slice each breast into ½-inch slices on the diagonal, and serve immediately.

4 (7-ounce) duck breast halves

1 cup hoisin sauce *

½ cup mirin* or sherry

1 tablespoon Chinese chile paste with garlic *

¼ cup chopped cilantro

¼ cup chopped scallions

3 garlic cloves, peeled and minced

2 tablespoons grated fresh ginger

Salt and freshly ground black pepper to taste

* Available in the Asian aisle of most supermarkets and in specialty markets.

Asian Duck Breast

6–8 turkey breast cutlets, about ½ inch thick

¼ cup olive oil, divided

2 teaspoons Italian seasoning

Salt and freshly ground black pepper to taste

¼ cup balsamic vinegar

2 garlic cloves, peeled and minced

1 tablespoon chopped fresh oregano or 1 teaspoon dried

1½ cups chopped fresh plum tomatoes

1 cup finely chopped radicchio

2 scallions, white parts only, trimmed and chopped

Turkey Cutlets Ensalata

Yield: 6–8 servings | Active time: 15 minutes | Start to finish: 35 minutes

1. Prepare a hot grill according to the instructions given in Chapter 1.

2. Rinse turkey and pat dry with paper towels. Rub cutlets with 1 tablespoon olive oil, and sprinkle with Italian seasoning, salt, and pepper. Set aside. Combine vinegar, garlic, oregano, salt, and pepper in a jar with a tight-fitting lid, and shake well. Add remaining olive oil, and shake well again.

3. Grill turkey for 2–3 minutes per side, uncovered, or until turkey is cooked through and no longer pink. Remove turkey from the grill, and keep warm.

4. Combine tomatoes, radicchio, and scallions in a mixing bowl. Toss with dressing. To serve, top each cutlet with a portion of salad mixture, and serve immediately.

Note: The dressing can be prepared up to 1 day in advance and refrigerated, tightly covered. Allow it to reach room temperature before using.

Chapter 8

Beef and Venison

Of course there is a chapter in this book about cooking beef—after all, steaks on the grill are part and parcel of life if you list yourself among the ranks of carnivores. Even on a gas grill, the aroma and flavor of a grilled steak is unsurpassed. It is only in the past few decades that farm-raised game has been available to home cooks and not just restaurant chefs. That has placed such culinary wonders as lean, healthful venison in supermarkets, and you will find some recipes for that meat in this chapter, too.

Steak Tacos with Pico de Gallo

Yield: 6–8 servings | Active time: 20 minutes | Start to finish: 3½ hours, including 3 hours for marinating

1. Rinse flank steak and pat dry with paper towels. Score steak with a paring knife lightly in a diamond pattern on both sides. Combine garlic, chile, cilantro, orange juice, lime juice, salt, and pepper in a blender or food processor fitted with a steel blade. Puree until smooth. Add olive oil, and mix well. Pour marinade into a heavy resealable plastic bag, add steak, and marinate, refrigerated, for a minimum of 3 hours, up to 8 hours, turning the bag occasionally.

2. Prepare a hot grill according to the instructions given in Chapter 1.

3. Remove staek from marinade, and discard marinade. Grill steak, uncovered if using a charcoal grill, for 3–4 minutes per side for medium-rare, or to desired doneness. Allow steak to rest for 5 minutes, then carve into slices. While steak rests, warm tortillas on the grill. Divide beef on top of tortillas, and serve immediately, passing bowls of lettuce, onion, cheese, and Pico de Gallo separately.

Note: The marinade can be prepared up to one day in advance and refrigerated, tightly covered.

1 (2-pound) flank steak

4 garlic cloves, peeled

1 jalapeño or serrano chile, stemmed

½ cup firmly packed fresh cilantro leaves

⅓ cup freshly squeezed orange juice

¼ cup freshly squeezed lime juice

Salt and freshly ground black pepper to taste

½ cup olive oil

12–16 (6-inch) corn tortillas

Shredded iceberg lettuce, chopped onion, grated Monterey Jack cheese, and Pico de Gallo (see recipe page 107)

4–6 (10-ounce) New York strip or boneless rib eye steaks

Salt and freshly ground black pepper to taste

¼ cup Worcestershire sauce

1 tablespoon red wine vinegar

1 tablespoon Dijon mustard

2 large shallots, peeled and minced

2 garlic cloves, peeled and minced

3 tablespoons chopped fresh parsley

2 tablespoons chopped fresh oregano or 2 teaspoons dried

1 tablespoon chopped fresh rosemary or 1 teaspoon dried

1 tablespoon fresh thyme or 1 teaspoon dried

⅓ cup extra-virgin olive oil

Steak with Herb Sauce

Yield: 4–6 servings | Active time: 25 minutes | Start to finish: 40 minutes

1. Prepare a dual-temperature hot-and-medium grill according to the instructions given in Chapter 1. Rinse steaks and pat dry with paper towels. Sprinkle steaks with salt and pepper.

2. Combine Worcestershire sauce, vinegar, mustard, shallots, garlic, parsley, oregano, rosemary, thyme, salt, and pepper in a jar with a tight-fitting lid, and shake well. Add olive oil, and shake well again. Set aside.

3. Sear steaks over the hot side of the grill for 2–3 minutes per side, uncovered if using a charcoal grill. Transfer steaks to the cooler side of the grill and cook for an additional 5–7 minutes, uncovered if using a charcoal grill, or to desired doneness. Allow steaks to rest for 5 minutes. To serve, slice steaks into ¾-inch slices and top with sauce. Serve immediately.

Note: The sauce can be prepared up to 1 day in advance and refrigerated, tightly covered. Allow it to reach room temperature before using.

---

1 (2-pound) flank steak

¼ cup soy sauce

¼ cup dry red wine

1 tablespoon Dijon mustard

2 tablespoons chopped fresh basil, preferably Thai basil, or 2 teaspoons dried

6 garlic cloves, peeled and minced

2 tablespoons chopped fresh cilantro

½ teaspoon crushed red pepper flakes or to taste

Salt to taste

¼ cup olive oil

Garlicky Flank Steak

Yield: 4–6 servings | Active time: 15 minutes | Start to finish: 3½ hours, including 3 hours for marinating

1. Rinse flank steak and pat dry with paper towels. Score steak with a paring knife on both sides in a diamond pattern ½ inch deep. Combine soy sauce, wine, mustard, basil, garlic, cilantro, red pepper flakes, and salt in a heavy resealable plastic bag. Mix well, add olive oil, and mix well again. Add steak to marinade and marinate, refrigerated, for a minimum of 3 hours and up to 8 hours, turning the bag occasionally.

2. Prepare a hot grill according to the instructions given in Chapter 1.

3. Grill steak, uncovered if using a charcoal grill, for 3–4 minutes per side for medium-rare or to desired doneness. Allow steak to rest for 5 minutes, then carve into slices. Serve immediately.

Note: The marinade can be prepared up to 1 day in advance and refrigerated, tightly covered.

Steak with Marsala Mushroom Sauce

Yield: 4–6 servings | Active time: 20 minutes | Start to finish: 45 minutes

1. Prepare a dual-temperature hot-and-medium grill according to the instructions given in Chapter 1. Rinse steaks and pat dry with paper towels. Sprinkle steaks with salt and pepper.

2. Heat oil and butter in a large skillet over medium-high heat. Add shallots and garlic and cook, stirring frequently, for 3 minutes, or until shallots are translucent. Add mushrooms and cook, stirring frequently, for 5 minutes. Add marsala, stock, parsley, and thyme. Bring to a boil, and cook, stirring occasionally, until sauce is reduced by two-thirds. Season to taste with salt and pepper, and keep warm.

3. Sear steaks over the hot side of the grill for 2–3 minutes per side, uncovered if using a charcoal grill. Transfer steaks to the cooler side of the grill and cook for an additional 5–7 minutes, uncovered if using a charcoal grill, or to desired doneness. Allow steaks to rest for 5 minutes. To serve, slice steaks into ¾-inch slices and top with sauce. Serve immediately.

VARIATION: *Veal loin chops are also delicious with this sauce, as are chicken breasts.*

Note: The sauce can be prepared up to 1 day in advance and refrigerated, tightly covered. Reheat it over low heat before using.

4–6 (10-ounce) New York strip or boneless rib eye steaks

Salt and freshly ground black pepper to taste

¼ cup olive oil

3 tablespoons unsalted butter

3 shallots, peeled and minced

3 garlic cloves, peeled and minced

¾ pound mushrooms, wiped with a damp paper towel and sliced

1½ cups marsala wine

½ cup beef stock

¼ cup chopped fresh parsley

1 tablespoon fresh thyme or 1 teaspoon dried

Steak with Marsala Mushroom Sauce

2 (2-pound) T-bone or
Porterhouse steaks,
about 2 inches thick

¼ cup olive oil

5 garlic cloves, peeled and
minced

2 tablespoons chopped
fresh rosemary or 2
teaspoons dried

Salt and freshly ground
black pepper to taste

4 tablespoons (½ stick)
unsalted butter, softened

¼ cup freshly grated
Parmesan cheese

1 tablespoon Spanish
smoked paprika

2 teaspoons Dijon mustard

Steak with Tuscan Parmesan Butter

Yield: 4–6 servings | Active time: 20 minutes | Start to finish: 45 minutes

1. Prepare a dual-temperature hot-and-medium grill according to the instructions given in Chapter 1. Rinse steak and pat dry with paper towels.

2. Combine olive oil, garlic, rosemary, salt, and pepper in a small bowl, and mix well. Rub mixture on both sides of steaks, and set aside.

3. Combine butter, Parmesan, paprika, mustard, salt, and pepper in another small bowl, and mix well. Form mixture into a log with a sheet of plastic wrap, and chill until ready to use.

4. Sear steaks over the hot side of the grill for 2–3 minutes per side, uncovered if using a charcoal grill. Transfer steaks to the cooler side of the grill and cook for an additional 6–8 minutes, uncovered if using a charcoal grill, for rare or to desired doneness. Allow steaks to rest for 5 minutes. To serve, slice steaks into ¾-inch slices and top each serving with 1 pat of seasoned butter. Serve immediately.

Note: The butter topping can be prepared up to 1 day in advance and refrigerated, tightly covered.

Steak with Tuscan Parmesan Butter

Steak, Potato, and Mushroom Kebabs

Yield: 4–6 servings | Active time: 25 minutes | Start to finish: 3 hours, including 2 hours for marinating

1. Soak bamboo skewers in warm water to cover. Rinse beef and pat dry with paper towels. Cut beef into 1½-inch cubes. Remove and discard mushroom stems. Wipe mushrooms clean with a damp paper towel. Cut each mushroom into 8 chunks.

2. Combine wine, vinegar, garlic, rosemary, thyme, salt, and pepper in a heavy resealable plastic bag, and mix well. Add olive oil, and mix well again. Add beef and mushrooms to the bag, and marinate, refrigerated, for 2 hours or up to 4 hours, turning the bag occasionally.

3. Place potatoes in a saucepan of salted water. Bring to a boil over high heat, and boil potatoes for 10 minutes, or until barely tender. Drain potatoes, and plunge into ice water to stop the cooking. When cool enough to handle, cut potatoes in half, or quarter them if larger than 3 inches in diameter. Set aside.

5. Prepare a dual-temperature hot-and-medium grill according to the instructions given in Chapter 1.

6. Remove meat and mushrooms from marinade, and discard marinade. Thread beef, mushroom sections, and potatoes onto 2 parallel skewers.

7. Sear kebabs on the hot side of the grill for 1½ minutes, turning them in quarter turns, uncovered if using a charcoal grill, on the hot side of the grill. Then transfer skewers to cooler side of the grill, and cook for a total of 6 minutes more for medium-rare, or to desired doneness. Serve immediately.

VARIATION: *Cubes of boneless leg of lamb are also delicious with this recipe.*

Note: The marinade can be prepared and the potatoes can be boiled 1 day in advance and refrigerated, tightly covered.

8–12 (8-inch) bamboo skewers
2 pounds sirloin tips
2 large portobello mushrooms
¾ cup dry red wine
¼ cup balsamic vinegar
2 garlic cloves, peeled and minced
3 tablespoons chopped fresh rosemary or 1 tablespoon dried
1 tablespoon fresh thyme or 1 teaspoon dried
Salt and freshly ground black pepper to taste
⅓ cup olive oil
1 pound small new potatoes, scrubbed

4–6 (6-ounce) boneless venison steaks, cut from the loin

Salt and freshly ground black pepper to taste

1 tablespoon dried sage

¾ cup port

1 cup beef stock

1 tablespoon fresh thyme, or 1 teaspoon dried

1 tablespoon chopped fresh parsley

½ cup whole berry cranberry sauce

3 tablespoons unsalted butter, cut into small pieces

Medallions of Venison with Cranberries

Yield: 4–6 servings | Active time: 20 minutes | Start to finish: 40 minutes

1. Prepare a hot grill according to the instructions given in Chapter 1. Rinse venison and pat dry with paper towels. Place venison between 2 sheets of plastic wrap and pound to an even thickness of ⅓ inch. Sprinkle venison with salt and pepper, and rub with sage.

2. Pour port into a heavy 1-quart saucepan, and bring to a boil over medium-high heat. Boil until reduced by half, stirring occasionally. Add stock, thyme, parsley, and cranberry sauce, and bring back to a boil. Boil until reduced by half, stirring occasionally. Whisk in butter, season with salt and pepper, and keep sauce warm.

3. Sear venison for 2 minutes per side, uncovered if using a charcoal grill, or until rare. Serve immediately, topped with sauce.

4–6 (6-ounce) boneless venison steaks, cut from the loin

3 cups dry red wine, divided

2 shallots, peeled and chopped

2 garlic cloves, peeled and minced

2 tablespoons chopped fresh parsley

1 tablespoon fresh thyme or 1 teaspoon dried

2 bay leaves

Salt and freshly ground black pepper to taste

½ cup olive oil

4 tablespoons (½ stick) unsalted butter, divided

2 tablespoons vegetable oil

6 scallions, white parts only, trimmed and chopped

2 tablespoons brandy

Venison Steaks with Red Wine Sauce

Yield: 4–6 servings | Active time: 20 minutes | Start to finish: 8½ hours, including 8 hours for marinating

1. Rinse venison and pat dry with paper towels. Place venison between 2 sheets of plastic wrap and pound to an even thickness of ⅓ inch. Combine 1½ cups wine, shallots, garlic, parsley, thyme, bay leaves, salt, and pepper in a heavy resealable plastic bag, and mix well. Add olive oil, and mix well again. Add venison, and marinate, refrigerated, for at least 8 hours or up to 24 hours, turning the bag occasionally.

2. Prepare a hot grill according to the instructions given in Chapter 1.

3. Heat 2 tablespoons butter and vegetable oil in a saucepan over medium-high heat. Add scallions and cook, stirring frequently, for 2 minutes, or until scallions are translucent. Raise the heat to high, and add remaining 1½ cups wine and brandy. Reduce over high heat, stirring occasionally, until only ⅔ cup remains. Cut remaining butter into small pieces, and whisk butter into sauce. Season to taste with salt and pepper, and set aside.

4. Remove venison from marinade and discard marinade. Sear venison for 2–3 minutes per side, uncovered if using a charcoal grill. Top steaks with sauce, and serve immediately.

Note: The sauce can be prepared up to 1 day in advance and refrigerated, tightly covered. Reheat it over low heat before using.

Chapter 9

Lamb, Pork, and Veal

During the mid-twentieth century, when I was first exposed to fine dining, the white-tablecloth restaurants in this country were termed "continental," and one of the dishes of note was always shish kebab; sometimes it even arrived on swords rather than skewers. It was one of the few ways that many Americans enjoyed eating lamb. The same menu would frequently include some Italian veal dishes, although most likely covered in cheese, and little pork other than the occasional ham steak topped with a ring of canned pineapple.

But all of that has changed, and while beef will probably always remain the king of red meats, lamb is now growing in popularity due to its rich, rosy flavor. And both pork and veal, now dubbed "the other white meats," are flavorful and tender alternatives to chicken.

Years ago there were butcher shops as well as butchers in every store to fulfill any special needs you might have for a cut of meat. However, that is no longer the case, so there are a few tasks formerly performed by butchers that it is good to know how to do. Here are the two main ones:

- **Trimming a pork tenderloin.** Pork tenderloins usually come in packages of two, each weighing between ¾ pound and 1 pound. The first task is to use the blade of a paring knife to scrape away the fat and very thin membrane coating the entire tenderloin. After this is accomplished you will see a stripe of iridescent white running from about halfway up the tenderloin to the thick end; this is the silver skin, and it should be removed so that the tenderloin will cook without curling. It is also very tough and gristly if eaten. Hold the end of the silver skin at the thin end with one hand, and insert a paring knife under it. Scrape it away from the meat, and repeat the process until all the silver skin has been removed.

- **Butterflying a leg of lamb.** It is now rather easy to find a boneless leg of lamb, but to grill successfully it has to lay much flatter on the grill. Remove the netting encasing it, or cut the strings creating its cylindrical shape. Roll out the meat, and you will have parts of various thicknesses ranging from almost no meat to an area about 6 inches thick. Start by cutting away large areas of fat, and trim the solid fat coating, called the fell, on what would have been the top of the leg to an even thickness of ¼ inch. Holding your knife parallel to the counter, start slicing the thicker areas of the lamb, pulling them open as if you were rolling out a sheet of piecrust. When all the meat is basically flat, cover the lamb with a sheet of plastic wrap, and pound it to an even thickness of 2 inches with the bottom of a small skillet or the flat side of a meat mallet.

2 (8-rib) racks of lamb, cut into 1-rib serving pieces

½ cup olive oil

1 cup chopped fresh cilantro

4 garlic cloves, peeled and minced

1 tablespoon paprika

1 tablespoon ground coriander

1 teaspoon ground cumin

Salt and freshly ground black pepper to taste

Moroccan Lamb Chops

Yield: 4–6 servings | Active time: 15 minutes | Start to finish: 1¼ hours, including 1 hour for marinating

1. Rinse lamb and pat dry with paper towels. Combine olive oil, cilantro, garlic, paprika, coriander, cumin, salt, and pepper in a heavy resealable plastic bag, and mix well. Add chops, coating them well with mixture. Marinate chops at room temperature for 1 hour, turning the bag occasionally, or up to 6 hours refrigerated.

2. Prepare a medium-hot grill according to the instructions given in Chapter 1. Remove lamb chops from marinade, and discard marinade.

3. Grill chops, covered, for 3 minutes per side for medium-rare or to desired doneness. Serve immediately.

Note: The lamb chops can be grilled up to 1 day in advance and refrigerated, tightly covered. Reheat them in a single layer in a 450°F oven for 3 minutes per side, or until heated through.

Moroccan Lamb Chops

Basque Lamb and Potato Kebabs

Yield: 6–8 servings | Active time: 20 minutes | Start to finish: 40 minutes

1. Soak bamboo skewers in warm water to cover, and prepare a medium-hot grill according to the instructions given in Chapter 1. Bring a pot of salted water to a boil, and boil potato cubes for 10–12 minutes, or until almost tender. Drain, and set aside.

2. Rinse lamb, and pat dry with paper towels. Combine olive oil, paprika, thyme, garlic, salt, and pepper in a low bowl. Add lamb and potato cubes, and toss gently to coat evenly.

3. Thread lamb and potatoes onto 2 parallel skewers. Grill lamb, uncovered, for 2–3 minutes per side for medium-rare, turning it in quarter turns, basting with sauce. Serve immediately on a bed of Basque Tomato Sauce.

Note: The lamb and potato skewers can be prepared up to 6 hours in advance and refrigerated, tightly covered.

12–16 (8-inch) bamboo skewers

18 small red-skinned potatoes, cut into 1-inch cubes

3 pounds boneless leg of lamb, cut into 1-inch cubes

½ cup olive oil

3 tablespoons smoked Spanish paprika

1 tablespoon dried thyme

3 garlic cloves, peeled and minced

Salt and freshly ground black pepper to taste

2 cups Basque Tomato Sauce (recipe on page 17)

Middle Eastern Lamb Kebabs

Middle Eastern Lamb Kebabs with Greek Feta Sauce

Yield: 6–8 servings | Active time: 20 minutes | Start to finish: 1½ hours, including 1 hour for marinating

1. Rinse lamb, and pat dry with paper towels. Combine wine, shallots, garlic, oregano, cinnamon, salt, and pepper in a heavy resealable plastic bag, and mix well. Add olive oil, and mix well again. Add lamb, and marinate for 1 hour at room temperature or up to 6 hours refrigerated, turning the bag occasionally.

2. Soak bamboo skewers in warm water to cover, and prepare a medium-hot grill according to the instructions given in Chapter 1.

3. Remove lamb from marinade, and discard marinade. Thread lamb onto 2 parallel skewers. Grill lamb, uncovered, for 2–3 minutes per side, turning it in quarter turns, for medium-rare. Serve immediately, passing Greek Feta Sauce separately.

3 pounds boneless leg of lamb, fat trimmed, cut into 1-inch cubes

1 cup dry red wine

2 shallots, peeled and chopped

4 garlic cloves, peeled and minced

2 tablespoons dried oregano

½ teaspoon ground cinnamon

Salt and freshly ground black pepper to taste

½ cup olive oil

12–16 (8-inch) bamboo skewers

Greek Feta Sauce (recipe on page 18)

2 (¾-pound) pork tenderloins, trimmed of fat and silver skin as described above

½ cup light molasses

⅓ cup cider vinegar

¼ cup Dijon mustard

3 garlic cloves, peeled and minced

1 shallot, peeled and chopped

1 tablespoon dried sage

Salt and freshly ground black pepper to taste

German-style Pork Tenderloin

Yield: 4–6 servings | Active time: 20 minutes | Start to finish: 4½ hours, including 4 hours for marinating

1. Rinse pork and pat dry with paper towels. Combine molasses, vinegar, mustard, garlic, shallot, sage, salt, and pepper in a mixing bowl and whisk well.

2. Place pork in a heavy resealable plastic bag, and pour marinade over pork. Marinate pork, refrigerated, for a minimum of 4 hours and up to 8 hours, turning the bag occasionally.

3. Prepare a dual-temperature hot-and-medium grill according to the instructions given in Chapter 1.

4. Remove pork from marinade, and transfer marinade to a small saucepan. Bring marinade to a boil over medium-high heat, stirring occasionally. Reduce the heat to low, and simmer sauce for 5 minutes.

5. Grill pork, uncovered if using a charcoal grill, on the hot side of the grill for 2–3 minutes per side, turning it in quarter turns, and then move pork to the cooler side of the grill. Grill for an additional 5–6 minutes per side for medium. Allow pork to rest for 5 minutes, then slice pork on the diagonal into ½-inch slices, and pass sauce separately.

6–8 (1-inch-thick) bone-in pork chops

Salt and freshly ground black pepper to taste

5 garlic cloves, peeled and minced, divided

3 tablespoons dried sage

Pinch of ground allspice

2 ripe mangoes, peeled and coarsely chopped

⅓ cup freshly squeezed lime juice

1 jalapeño or serrano chile, seeds and ribs removed, and diced

1 tablespoon grated orange zest

2 tablespoons olive oil

3 tablespoons chopped fresh cilantro

Pork Chops with Mango Sauce

Yield: 6–8 servings | Active time: 15 minutes | Start to finish: 35 minutes

1. Prepare a dual-temperature hot-and-medium grill according to the instructions given in Chapter 1.

2. Rinse pork chops and pat dry with paper towels. Sprinkle pork chops with salt and pepper. Combine 2 garlic cloves, sage, and allspice in a small bowl, and rub mixture on both sides of chops.

3. Combine mangoes, lime juice, remaining garlic, chile, orange zest, and olive oil in a food processor fitted with a steel blade or in a blender. Puree until smooth. Stir in cilantro, and season to taste with salt and pepper. Set aside.

4. Grill chops, uncovered if using a charcoal grill, on the hot side of the grill for 2–3 minutes per side and then move them to the cooler side of the grill. Grill for an additional 5–6 minutes per side for medium. Allow chops to rest for 5 minutes, then serve immediately, passing sauce separately.

Note: The sauce can be made up to 2 days in advance and refrigerated, tightly covered. Bring it to room temperature before using.

Smoky Pork Chops with Apples
Yield: 6 servings | Active time: 20 minutes | Start to finish: 25 hours, including 24 hours for brining

1. Rinse pork and pat dry with paper towels. Place pork in a 1-gallon heavy resealable plastic bag. Add water, ¼ cup honey, salt, and pepper. Marinate pork, refrigerated, for 24 hours, turning the bag occasionally.

2. Prepare a medium-hot grill according to the instructions given in Chapter 1. If using a charcoal grill, soak wood chips in water for 30 minutes. If using a gas grill, create a packet of wood chips as described in Chapter 1.

3. Just prior to grilling pork, heat butter in a large skillet over medium heat. Combine remaining honey and cinnamon. Add apples to the pan, and baste with honey mixture. Cook apples over medium heat, turning gently with tongs, for 6 minutes, or until cooked but still retaining texture. Remove the pan from the heat and keep apples warm.

4. Remove pork from brine, and discard brine. Place wood chips on the grill, and cook pork for 6–8 minutes per side, covered, or until just slightly pink in the center. To serve, top each pork chop with some apple slices.

Note: The apples can be prepared 1 day in advance and refrigerated, tightly covered. Reheat them over low heat, stirring gently occasionally.

2 pounds boneless pork loin, cut into 6 slices
1 cup cold water
½ cup honey, divided
2 tablespoons kosher salt
Freshly ground black pepper to taste
1 cup apple wood chips
2 tablespoons unsalted butter
1 teaspoon ground cinnamon
3 cooking apples, such as Granny Smith, cored and cut into 12 slices each

2 cups hickory or mesquite chips

2 racks pork spareribs (about 6½ pounds)

¼ cup Aromatic Herb and Spice Rub (recipe on page 8), or any spice rub of your choice

2 cups My Favorite Barbecue Sauce (recipe on page 16), or any barbecue sauce of your choice

Basic All-American Barbecued Ribs

Yield: 4–6 servings | Active time: 20 minutes | Start to finish: 4 hours

1. If using a charcoal grill, soak hickory or mesquite chips in water for 30 minutes. If using a gas grill, create a packet for wood chips as described in Chapter 1. Rinse ribs, and pat dry with paper towels. Cut each rack in half. Rub both sides of ribs with spice rub, and allow to sit at room temperature while the grill heats.

2. Prepare a grill for indirect cooking as described in Chapter 1, pushing the coals to one side rather than around the periphery if using a charcoal grill, and lighting the burners on only one side if using a gas grill.

3. Drain wood chips, and sprinkle on coals, or place packet of wood chips under grate on burners. Place ribs on the cool side of the grill, and cook for 2 hours, covered, turning the racks every 30 minutes to cook evenly. Add more charcoal to fire after 1 hour.

4. Move ribs to hot part of grill, and baste with barbecue sauce. Cook for 5–7 minutes per side, or until ribs are browned. Remove ribs from the grill, wrap in heavy-duty aluminum foil, and let them rest for 45 minutes.

5. Reheat foil packets on the cool side of the grill, if necessary, then cut ribs into servings, and serve immediately. Pass extra sauce separately.

Basic All-American Barbecued Ribs

Lemon-Herb Veal Chops

Lemon-Herb Veal Chops

Yield: 6 servings | Active time: 15 minutes | Start to finish: 4½ hours, including 4 hours for marinating

1. Rinse veal chops and pat dry with paper towels. Combine lemon juice with ¼ cup parsley, 2 tablespoons rosemary, thyme, 2 garlic cloves, shallot, salt, and pepper in a heavy resealable plastic bag, and mix well. Add olive oil, and mix well again. Add chops and marinate, refrigerated, for 4–6 hours, turning the bag occasionally.

2. While chops are marinating, combine remaining parsley, remaining rosemary, remaining garlic, and lemon zest in a small bowl. Mix well, and set aside.

3. Prepare a dual-temperature hot-and-medium grill according to the instructions given in Chapter 1.

4. Remove chops from marinade, discard marinade, and pat chops dry with paper towels. Grill chops on the hot side of the grill, uncovered if using a charcoal grill, for 3–4 minutes per side, then move them to the cooler side of the grill and cook for 4–5 minutes per side for medium or to desired doneness. Transfer chops to a platter or individual plates, and allow chops to rest for 5 minutes. Then sprinkle each with a few teaspoons of topping, and serve immediately.

VARIATION: *Thick pork chops are also delicious when soaked in this marinade.*

6 (1-inch-thick) veal chops

⅓ cup freshly squeezed lemon juice

½ cup chopped fresh parsley, divided

¼ cup chopped fresh rosemary, divided

1 tablespoons fresh thyme or 1 teaspoon dried

3 garlic cloves, peeled and minced, divided

1 shallot, peeled and chopped

Salt and freshly ground black pepper to taste

½ cup olive oil

1 tablespoon grated lemon zest

Chapter 10

Burgers of All Types

While burger was formerly synonymous with beef, that is no longer the case. Today, any food that is ground and eaten on a bun is lumped under the category of "burgers"—including lentils, various aquatic species, and lots of poultry. Tose are among the recipes you will find in this chapter.

1¾ pounds tuna fillets

3 scallions, white parts only, trimmed and chopped

2 garlic cloves, peeled and minced

2 tablespoons freshly grated ginger

2 tablespoons fish sauce (nam pla) *

1 tablespoon mirin* or sweet sherry

Salt and freshly ground black pepper to taste

1 tablespoon wasabi powder *

2 tablespoons cold water

⅔ cup mayonnaise

3 tablespoons finely chopped pickled ginger

2 teaspoons Asian sesame oil*

4–6 rolls of your choice, sliced in half

2 tablespoons vegetable oil

Lettuce and tomato

* Available in the Asian aisle of most supermarkets and in specialty markets.

Tuna Burgers with Wasabi Mayonnaise
Yield: 4–6 servings | Active time: 20 minutes | Start to finish: 2 hours

1. Rinse tuna and pat dry with paper towels, and cut into 1-inch pieces, discarding sinews. Place tuna cubes on a sheet of plastic wrap, and freeze for 20–30 minutes, or until firm but not solid. Chop tuna in a food processor fitted with a steel blade, using on-and-off pulsing. Place tuna in a mixing bowl and add scallions, garlic, ginger, fish sauce, mirin, salt, and pepper.

2. Form tuna mixture into 4–6 (¾-inch-thick) burgers. Cover burgers with plastic wrap, and refrigerate for at least 45 minutes.

3. Prepare a hot grill according to the instructions given in Chapter 1. While burgers chill, combine wasabi and water in a mixing bowl to form a paste. Add mayonnaise, pickled ginger, and sesame oil. Stir well, and refrigerate until ready to use.

4. Grill rolls cut side down until toasted. Rub burgers with oil, and grill for 2–3 minutes per side, uncovered if using a charcoal grill, for a rare burger or to desired doneness. Serve immediately on rolls with sauce, lettuce, tomato, and wasabi mayonnaise.

Note: The burgers can be formed up to 6 hours in advance and refrigerated, tightly covered.

Dilled Salmon Burgers

Yield: 4–6 servings | Active time: 20 minutes | Start to finish: 2 hours

1 (1½-pound) salmon fillet, skinned

¼ cup Dijon mustard, divided

¼ cup chopped fresh dill, divided

Salt and freshly ground black pepper to taste

¼ cup mayonnaise

¼ cup sour cream

4–6 rolls of your choice, sliced in half

2 tablespoons vegetable oil

Lettuce, tomato, and thinly sliced red onion

1. Rinse salmon and pat dry with paper towels, and cut into 1-inch pieces. Place salmon cubes on a sheet of plastic wrap, and freeze for 20–30 minutes, until firm but not solid. Chop salmon in a food processor fitted with a steel blade, using on-and-off pulsing. Place salmon in a mixing bowl and add 2 tablespoons mustard and 2 tablespoons dill. Season to taste with salt and pepper.

2. Form salmon mixture into 4–6 (¾-inch-thick) burgers. Cover burgers with plastic wrap, and refrigerate for at least 45 minutes.

3. Prepare a medium-hot grill according to the instructions given in Chapter 1. While burgers chill, combine mayonnaise and sour cream with remaining mustard and remaining dill. Stir well, and refrigerate until ready to use.

4. Grill rolls cut side down until toasted. Rub burgers with oil, and grill for 3 minutes per side, covered, for a medium-rare burger or to desired doneness. Serve immediately on rolls with sauce, lettuce, tomato, and onion slices.

VARIATION: *Tuna or a firm-fleshed white fish like cod or halibut can be substituted for the salmon.*

Note: The burgers can be formed up to 6 hours in advance and refrigerated, tightly covered.

Dilled Salmon Burgers

2 tablespoons vegetable oil

1 small onion, peeled and chopped

2 garlic cloves, peeled and minced

1 celery rib, rinsed, trimmed, and chopped

1 red bell pepper, seeds and ribs removed, and finely chopped

1½ pounds large shrimp (21–30 per pound), peeled and deveined

3 tablespoons chopped fresh chives

3 tablespoons chopped fresh parsley

½ teaspoon hot red pepper sauce or to taste

Cajun seasoning to taste

4–6 long submarine rolls, split in half

Lettuce, tomato, and tartar sauce

Hawaiian Shrimp Burgers

Yield: 4–6 servings | Active time: 20 minutes | Start to finish: 45 minutes

1. Prepare a dual-temperature hot-and-medium grill according to the instructions given in Chapter 1.

2. Heat oil in a large skillet over medium heat. Add onion, garlic, celery, and red bell pepper. Cook, stirring frequently, for 5–7 minutes, or until vegetables are soft. Scrape mixture into a mixing bowl.

3. Finely chop ½ pound shrimp, and add to the bowl. Puree remaining 1 pound shrimp in a food processor fitted with a steel blade. Add to the bowl, along with chives, parsley, hot red pepper sauce, and Cajun seasoning. Form mixture into 8–12 oval (½-inch-thick) patties.

4. Grill rolls cut-side down until toasted. Sear shrimp burgers, uncovered if using a charcoal grill, for 2 minutes per side over hot heat, and then cook for an additional 2 minutes per side over medium heat or until cooked through. Serve immediately on rolls with lettuce, tomato, and tartar sauce.

VARIATION: *Scallops or a firm-fleshed white fish such as cod or tilapia can be substituted for the shrimp. Serve immediately on rolls with lettuce, tomato, and tartar sauce.*

Note: The shrimp mixture can be prepared up to 1 day in advance and refrigerated, tightly covered.

Herbed Turkey Burgers

Yield: 4–6 servings | Active time: 15 minutes | Start to finish: 40 minutes

1¾ pounds ground turkey

1 Golden Delicious or Granny Smith apple, peeled, cored, and grated

3 tablespoons chopped fresh sage or 1 tablespoon dried

¼ teaspoon ground allspice

Salt and freshly ground black pepper to taste

4–6 rolls of your choice, sliced in half

Lettuce, tomato, and thinly sliced red onion

1. Prepare a dual-temperature hot-and-medium grill according to the instructions given in Chapter 1.

2. Combine turkey with apple, sage, and allspice. Season to taste with salt and pepper. Form mixture into 4–6 (¾-inch-thick) burgers.

3. Grill rolls cut-side down on the hot side of the grill until toasted. Sear burgers over high heat for 2 minutes per side, uncovered if using a charcoal grill, and then transfer burgers to the cooler side of the grill. Continue to cook, covered, for 3–5 minutes per side or until burgers register 160°F on an instant-read thermometer and are cooked through and no longer pink. Serve immediately on rolls with lettuce, tomato, and red onion.

VARIATION: *Ground pork or ground veal can be substituted for the turkey. Cook these meats to desired doneness.*

Note: The turkey mixture can be prepared up to 1 day in advance and refrigerated, tightly covered.

Apple Cranberry Turkey Burgers

Yield: 4–6 servings | Active time: 15 minutes | Start to finish: 40 minutes

1¾ pounds ground turkey

1 Golden Delicious apple, peeled, cored, and grated

2 teaspoons dry mustard, divided

½ teaspoon dried thyme

Salt and freshly ground black pepper to taste

½ cup barbecue sauce

½ cup pure maple syrup

½ cup cider vinegar

¼ cup dried cranberries

1 teaspoon grated lemon zest

½ teaspoon ground cinnamon

½ teaspoon ground ginger

4–6 rolls of your choice, sliced in half

Lettuce, tomato, and thinly sliced red onion

1. Prepare a dual-temperature hot-and-medium grill according to the instructions given in Chapter 1.

2. Combine turkey with apple, 1 teaspoon dry mustard, and thyme in a mixing bowl. Season to taste with salt and pepper. Form mixture into 4–6 (¾-inch-thick) burgers.

3. Combine barbecue sauce, maple syrup, cider vinegar, dried cranberries, lemon zest, cinnamon, ginger, and remaining 1 teaspoon mustard in a small saucepan. Bring to a boil over medium-high heat, stirring occasionally. Reduce the heat to low, and simmer sauce for 3 minutes. Divide sauce into 2 small bowls.

4. Grill rolls cut-side down on the hot side of the grill until toasted. Sear burgers over high heat for 2 minutes per side, uncovered if using a charcoal grill, and then transfer burgers to the cooler side of the grill. Continue to cook, covered, basting with sauce every 2 minutes, for 3–5 minutes per side or until burgers register 160°F on an instant-read thermometer and are cooked through and no longer pink. Do not baste for the last 2 minutes, and discard basting sauce. Serve immediately on rolls with lettuce, tomato, and red onion. Pass second bowl of sauce separately.

VARIATION: *Ground pork or ground veal can be substituted for the turkey. Cook these meats to desired doneness.*

Note: Both the turkey mixture and the sauce can be prepared up to 1 day in advance and refrigerated, tightly covered.

1 cup mayonnaise

1 cup tightly packed chopped fresh basil

¼ cup chopped fresh parsley

¼ cup small capers, drained and rinsed

2 garlic cloves, peeled and minced

1 large shallot, peeled and chopped

2 teaspoons herbes de Provence

Salt and freshly ground black pepper to taste

1¾ pounds ground turkey

4–6 rolls of your choice, sliced in half

Lettuce, tomato, and thinly sliced red onion

Turkey Burgers Provençal

Yield: 4–6 servings | Active time: 15 minutes | Start to finish: 45 minutes

1. Prepare a dual-temperature hot-and-medium grill according to the instructions given in Chapter 1.

2. Combine mayonnaise, basil, parsley, capers, garlic, shallot, herbes de Provence, salt, and pepper in a mixing bowl, and stir well.

3. Combine ½ cup mayonnaise mixture and turkey in a mixing bowl, and mix gently. Form mixture into 4–6 (¾-inch-thick) burgers.

4. Grill rolls on the hot side of the grill, cut-side down, until toasted. Sear burgers over high heat for 2 minutes per side, uncovered if using a charcoal grill, and then transfer burgers to the cooler side of the grill. Continue to cook, covered, for 3–5 minutes per side or until burgers register 160°F on an instant-read thermometer and are cooked through and no longer pink.

5. Serve immediately with remaining mayonnaise mixture, lettuce, tomato, and onion.

VARIATION: *Ground pork or ground veal can be substituted for the turkey. Cook these meats to desired doneness.*

Note: The turkey mixture can be prepared up to 1 day in advance and refrigerated, tightly covered.

Beef and Chorizo Burgers

Yield: 4–6 servings | Active time: 15 minutes | Start to finish: 40 minutes

1. Prepare a medium-hot grill according to the instructions given in Chapter 1.

2. Remove casings from chorizo, if necessary, and chop chorizo finely in a food processor fitted with a steel blade using on-and-off pulsing. Combine chorizo, ground chuck, shallots, 3 garlic cloves, cilantro, chili powder, cumin, and oregano in a mixing bowl. Season to taste with salt and cayenne. Mix well, and form mixture into 8–12 (⅓-inch-thick) patties. Place cheese on half of patties, and top with remaining patties. Press together gently to enclose cheese. Press with your thumb in the center of each burger to form an indentation; this keeps the burgers from creating a dome in the center.

3. Combine mayonnaise, remaining garlic, green chiles, and lime juice in a small bowl. Season with salt and cayenne to taste, and stir well. Set aside.

4. Grill rolls cut-side down until toasted. Grill burgers beginning with the side with the indentation up, uncovered if using a charcoal grill, for a total time of 4–6 minutes per side or to an internal temperature of 125°F for medium-rare or to desired doneness. To serve, place burgers on bottom half of rolls and top each with mayonnaise. Serve immediately with lettuce, tomato, and red onion.

VARIATION: *Ground turkey can be substituted for the beef. Cook burgers to an internal temperature of 160°F on an instant-read thermometer or until cooked through and no longer pink.*

Note: The beef mixture can be prepared up to 1 day in advance and refrigerated, tightly covered.

½ pound chorizo

1 pound ground chuck

2 shallots, peeled and finely chopped

4 garlic cloves, peeled and minced, divided

3 tablespoons chopped fresh cilantro

2 tablespoons chili powder

2 teaspoon ground cumin

1 teaspoon dried oregano

Salt and cayenne to taste

1 cup grated jalapeño Jack cheese

¾ cup mayonnaise

2 tablespoons diced canned mild green chiles, drained

1 tablespoon freshly squeezed lime juice

4 rolls of your choice, sliced in half

Lettuce, tomato slices, and thin slices of red onion

1¾ pounds ground chuck

¾ cup grated cheddar cheese

2 garlic cloves, peeled and minced

1 tablespoon fresh thyme or 1 teaspoon dried

Salt and freshly ground black pepper to taste

2 tablespoons unsalted butter

1 tablespoon olive oil

¼ pound fresh mushrooms, wiped with a damp paper towel and sliced

4-6 rolls of your choice, sliced in half

4-6 slices cheddar cheese

Lettuce, tomatoes, and thinly sliced red onion

Fancy Cheese Burger

Yield: 4-6 servings | Active time: 10 minutes | Start to finish: 40 minutes

1. Prepare a medium-hot grill according to the instructions given in Chapter 1.

2. Combine ground chuck, cheddar cheese, garlic, thyme, salt, and pepper in a mixing bowl, and mix gently. Form mixture into 4-6 (1-inch-thick) burgers. Press with your thumb in the center of each burger to form an indentation; this keeps the burgers from creating a dome in the center.

3. Heat butter and oil in a large skillet over medium-high heat. Add mushrooms and cook, stirring frequently, for 4-5 minutes, or until mushrooms are brown. Season to taste with salt and pepper, and set aside.

4. Grill rolls cut-side down until toasted. Grill burgers beginning with the side with the indentation up, uncovered if using a charcoal grill, for a total time of 4-6 minutes per side or to an internal temperature of 125°F for medium-rare or to desired doneness. Top burgers with sliced cheese for the last 2 minutes of grilling. Serve immediately with lettuce, tomato, and onion.

VARIATION: *Ground turkey can be substituted for the beef. Cook turkey to an internal temperature of 160°F on an instant-read thermometer or until cooked through and no longer pink. Also, blue cheese can be substituted for the cheddar cheese.*

Note: The beef mixture can be prepared up to 1 day in advance and refrigerated, tightly covered.

Fancy Cheese Burger

Chinese Pork Burgers

Yield: 4–6 servings | Active time: 20 minutes | Start to finish: 45 minutes

1. Prepare a medium-hot grill according to the instructions given in Chapter 1.

2. Combine pork, half of scallions, ginger, cilantro, garlic, soy sauce, sherry, water chestnuts, and pepper in a mixing bowl. Mix well and form into 4–6 (¾-inch-thick) burgers. Press with your thumb in the center of each burger to form an indentation; this keeps the burgers from creating a dome in the center. Combine mustard and hoisin sauce in a bowl, whisk well, and set aside.

3. Grill rolls cut-side down until toasted. Grill burgers beginning with the side with the indentation up, uncovered if using a charcoal grill, for a total time of 4–6 minutes per side or to an internal temperature of 150°F on an instant-read thermometer. Baste burgers with sauce for last 4 minutes of grilling.

4. Add remaining scallions to remaining basting sauce. Serve burgers immediately on rolls with lettuce and tomato. Pass sauce separately.

VARIATION: *Ground turkey or ground veal can be substituted for the pork. The turkey should be grilled to an internal temperature of 160°F or until cooked through and no longer pink.*

Note: The pork mixture can be prepared up to 1 day in advance and refrigerated, tightly covered.

1¾ pounds ground pork

12 scallions, white parts and 2 inches of green tops, rinsed, trimmed, and thinly sliced, divided

¼ cup grated fresh ginger

¼ cup chopped fresh cilantro

4 garlic cloves, peeled and minced

¼ cup soy sauce

2 tablespoons dry sherry

½ cup finely chopped water chestnuts

Freshly ground black pepper to taste

½ cup Dijon mustard

¼ cup hoisin sauce*

4–6 sesame rolls, sliced in half

Lettuce and tomato slices

* Available in the Asian aisle of most supermarkets and in specialty markets.

⅔ cup plain yogurt

1¾ pounds ground lamb

2 shallots, peeled and finely chopped

3 garlic cloves, peeled and minced

¼ cup chopped fresh parsley

2 tablespoons chopped fresh oregano or 2 teaspoons dried

1 tablespoon fresh thyme or 1 teaspoon dried

2 teaspoons ground cumin

Salt and freshly ground black pepper to taste

4–6 (8-inch) pita breads

½ cup finely chopped cucumber

2 ripe plum tomatoes, rinsed, cored, seeded, and finely chopped

Basque Lamb Burgers

Yield: 4–6 servings | Active time: 20 minutes | Start to finish: 40 minutes

1. Prepare a medium-hot grill according to the instructions given in Chapter 1.

2. Place yogurt in a strainer set over a mixing bowl. Shake strainer gently a few times, and allow yogurt to drain for at least 30 minutes at room temperature or up to 6 hours refrigerated. Discard whey from mixing bowl, and place yogurt in the bowl. Set aside.

3. Combine lamb, shallots, garlic, parsley, oregano, thyme, and cumin in a mixing bowl. Season to taste with salt and pepper. Mix well, and form mixture into 4–6 (1-inch-thick) burgers. Press with your thumb in the center of each burger to form an indentation; this keeps the burgers from creating a dome in the center.

4. Grill burgers beginning with the side with the indentation up, uncovered if using a charcoal grill, for a total time of 4–6 minutes per side or to an internal temperature of 125°F for medium-rare or to desired doneness. While burgers are grilling, combine drained yogurt, cucumber, and tomato a small bowl. Season to taste with salt and pepper.

5. To serve, cut top 1 inch off pita breads and place burgers inside. Spoon yogurt mixture on top of each burger in pita bread, and serve immediately.

VARIATION: *Ground beef can be substituted for the ground lamb.*

Note: The lamb mixture can be prepared up to 1 day in advance and refrigerated, tightly covered.

Middle Eastern Lentil Burgers

Yield: 4–6 servings | Active time: 20 minutes | Start to finish: 40 minutes

1. Place lentils in a 2-quart saucepan, cover with water, and add 1 teaspoon salt. Bring to a boil over medium-high heat, then reduce the heat to low and simmer lentils, covered, for 20 to 25 minutes or until cooked. Drain lentils, and place in a mixing bowl.

2. Prepare a medium-hot grill according to the instructions given in Chapter 1.

3. While lentils simmer, place pine nuts in a small dry skillet over medium heat. Toast nuts, shaking pan frequently, for 2–3 minutes, or until browned. Remove nuts from the pan, and set aside. Heat oil in the same small skillet over medium-high heat. Add onions and garlic, and cook, stirring frequently, for 3 minutes or until onion is translucent. Add coriander and cumin, and cook, stirring constantly, for 1 minute. Add onion mixture to lentils, and stir well.

4. Puree ½ cup pine nuts and 1 cup lentil mixture in a food processor fitted with a metal blade. Scrape mixture back into mixing bowl, and add remaining lentil mixture and remaining pine nuts. Season to taste with salt and pepper. Form mixture into 4–6 (¾-inch-thick) burgers.

5. Grill buns cut-side down until toasted. Grill burgers for 3 minutes per side, covered, turning them gently with a spatula. Serve immediately on buns with lettuce, tomato, and hummus.

Note: The lentil mixture can be prepared up to 1 day in advance and refrigerated, tightly covered. Allow it to reach room temperature before grilling the burgers.

2 cups lentils, picked over, rinsed, and drained

1 quart water

1 teaspoon salt

¾ cup pine nuts

2 tablespoons vegetable oil

1 medium onion, peeled and chopped

2 garlic cloves, peeled and minced

2 teaspoons ground coriander

1 teaspoon ground cumin

Salt and freshly ground black pepper to taste

6 sesame buns, sliced in half

Lettuce, tomato, and hummus

Chapter 11

Entree Salads

The recipes in this chapter can be considered a "two-fer." Entree salads—loaded with healthful fresh vegetables and some grilled protein—are also a great way to use up leftover grilled food from a previous meal. Stunning when they arrive at the table, the salads in this chapter are a complete meal, perhaps with the addition of some crusty bread. So do not be put off if the preparation time seems long; the salad is all you have to create.

1 cup apple wood chips

4–6 (12-ounce) trout, scaled, gutted with head left on

3 tablespoons olive oil

Salt and freshly ground black pepper to taste

½ cup sour cream

2 tablespoons prepared horseradish

2 tablespoons chopped fresh dill or 2 teaspoons dried

3 tablespoons freshly squeezed lemon juice

1 pint cherry tomatoes, rinsed and halved

½ English cucumber, cut into ⅓-inch dice

½ small red onion, peeled, halved lengthwise, and thinly sliced

4–6 cups chopped romaine, rinsed and dried

Trout Salad with Horseradish Dressing

Yield: 4–6 servings | Active time: 20 minutes | Start to finish: 40 minutes

1. Prepare a medium-hot grill according to the instructions given in Chapter 1. If using a charcoal grill, soak apple wood chips in water for 30 minutes. If using a gas grill, create a packet for wood chips as described in Chapter 1.

2. Rinse trout and pat dry with paper towels. Rub fish with oil, and sprinkle with salt and pepper. Set aside. Combine sour cream, horseradish, dill, lemon juice, salt, and pepper in a bowl, and whisk well. Refrigerate until ready to use.

3. Grill trout for 4 minutes per side, uncovered if using a charcoal grill, or until skin is crisp and flesh is no longer translucent.

4. To serve, combine tomatoes, cucumber, onion, and lettuce in a mixing bowl, and toss with enough dressing to coat vegetables lightly. Mound mixture onto a serving platter or individual plates, and top with trout. Serve immediately, passing extra dressing separately.

Note: The dressing can be made up to 1 day in advance and refrigerated, tightly covered.

Tuna Salad Niçoise

Yield: 4–6 servings | Active time: 20 minutes | Start to finish: 45 minutes

1. Place potatoes in a saucepan of salted water, and bring to a boil over high heat. Boil potatoes for 8–10 minutes, or until tender. Add green beans, and boil 2 minutes more. Drain vegetables, and rinse under cold running water. Refrigerate vegetables until cold.

2. Prepare a hot grill according to the instructions given in Chapter 1. Sprinkle tuna with salt and pepper, and place it on a sheet of plastic wrap in the freezer for 20–30 minutes.

3. Combine lemon juice, mustard, herbes de Provence, salt, and pepper in a jar with a tight-fitting lid, and shake well. Add olive oil, and shake well again.

4. Grill tuna steaks, uncovered if using a charcoal grill, for 2–3 minutes per side; the inside should remain almost raw, or cook to desired doneness. Slice steaks into ¼-inch slices against the grain, and set aside.

5. Toss salad greens with one-quarter of dressing, and arrange on a platter or individual plates. Top greens with tuna, potatoes, and green beans, and drizzle with additional dressing. Scatter olives, tomatoes, capers, parsley, and Parmesan over all, and serve immediately, passing remaining dressing separately.

Note: The vegetables can be boiled and the dressing can be made up to 1 day in advance and refrigerated, tightly covered. Bring the dressing to room temperature before using.

1 pound baby new potatoes, scrubbed and quartered

¼ pound green beans, rinsed and stemmed

3 (8-ounce) fresh tuna steaks, at least ¾ inch thick

Salt and freshly ground black pepper to taste

¼ cup freshly squeezed lemon juice

2 teaspoons Dijon mustard

1 teaspoon herbes de Provence

⅓ cup extra-virgin olive oil

4–6 cups mixed baby greens, rinsed and dried

½ cup pitted Niçoise or other oil-cured black olives, halved lengthwise

1 cup cherry tomatoes, rinsed and halved

2 tablespoons capers, drained and rinsed

¼ cup chopped fresh parsley leaves

¼ cup freshly grated Parmesan cheese

8–12 (8-inch) bamboo skewers

⅓ cup freshly squeezed lemon juice

4 garlic cloves, peeled and minced

2 tablespoons chopped fresh oregano or 2 teaspoons dried

2 tablespoons chopped fresh parsley

Salt and freshly ground black pepper to taste

½ cup extra-virgin olive oil, divided

1 pint cherry tomatoes, rinsed and halved

½ English cucumber, cut into ⅓-inch dice

½ small red onion, peeled, halved lengthwise, and thinly sliced

1½ pounds extra large (16–20 per pound) raw shrimp, peeled and deveined

1 orange or yellow bell pepper, seeds and ribs removed, and cut into ½-inch slices

4–6 cups baby spinach leaves, rinsed and dried

1 cup crumbled feta cheese

1 cup pitted kalamata olives

Greek Shrimp Salad

Yield: 4–6 servings | Active time: 20 minutes | Start to finish: 40 minutes

1. Soak bamboo skewers in warm water to cover, and prepare a medium-hot grill according to the instructions given in Chapter 1.

2. Combine lemon juice, garlic, oregano, parsley, salt, and pepper in a jar with a tight-fitting lid, and shake well. Add ⅓ cup olive oil, and shake well again.

3. Place tomatoes, cucumber, and red onion in a large mixing bowl. Toss with one-third of dressing, and refrigerate. Place shrimp in a heavy resealable plastic bag, and add one-third of dressing. Seal and turn bag to coat shrimp evenly. Marinate shrimp at room temperature for 10 minutes, or up to 30 minutes refrigerated.

4. Grill pepper slices, covered, for 3–5 minutes, or until soft. Remove peppers from the grill, and slice into strips. Add peppers to bowl with other vegetables.

5. Remove shrimp from marinade, and discard marinade. Divide shrimp into 4–6 groups, and thread each group onto 2 parallel skewers. Grill shrimp, covered, for 2 minutes per side, or until pink and cooked through. Remove shrimp from skewers.

6. To serve, place 1 portion spinach on each plate, and top with vegetables and shrimp. Sprinkle feta and olives on top, and serve immediately, passing remaining dressing separately.

VARIATION: *Any firm white-fleshed fish fillet such as halibut or cod will be just as delicious as the shrimp and will cook in the same amount of time. You can also substitute ¾-inch cubes of boneless, skinless chicken breast. The chicken should be marinated refrigerated for 1 hour, and the pieces should be cooked for 4–6 minutes per side, or until cooked through and no longer pink.*

Note: The dressing can be made up to 1 day in advance and refrigerated, tightly covered. Bring to room temperature before using.

Greek Shrimp Salad

1½ pounds boneless, skinless chicken breasts, rinsed and patted dry with paper towels

2 tablespoons freshly squeezed lime juice

2 tablespoons cider vinegar

1 tablespoon Dijon mustard

1 tablespoon honey

1 tablespoon chopped fresh parsley

2 teaspoons fresh thyme or ½ teaspoon dried

Salt and freshly ground black pepper to taste

½ cup olive oil

2 ripe peaches, peeled, stoned, and diced

½ small red onion, peeled and thinly sliced

6 cups mixed baby greens, rinsed and dried

Chicken and Peach Salad

Yield: 6–8 servings | Active time: 25 minutes | Start to finish: 35 minutes

1. Prepare a hot grill according to the instructions given in Chapter 1.

2. Trim chicken breasts of all visible fat, and pound to an even thickness of ½ inch between 2 sheets of plastic wrap. Place chicken breasts in a mixing bowl.

3. Combine lime juice, vinegar, mustard, honey, parsley, thyme, salt, and pepper in a jar with a tight-fitting lid, and shake well. Add olive oil, and shake well again.

4. Reserve half of dressing, and then mix remaining dressing into bowl with chicken breasts.

5. Grill chicken for 2–3 minutes per side, uncovered, or until chicken is cooked through and no longer pink. Remove chicken from the grill, and cut into thin slices against the grain.

6. To serve, combine peaches, onion, and greens in a mixing bowl, and toss with enough dressing to coat lightly. Mound mixture onto a serving platter or individual plates, and top with chicken slices. Serve immediately, passing extra dressing separately.

Note: The dressing can be made up to 1 day in advance and refrigerated, tightly covered. Bring to room temperature before using.

Grilled Chicken Caesar Salad

Grilled Chicken Caesar Salad

Yield: 6–8 servings | Active time: 25 minutes | Start to finish: 35 minutes

1. Prepare a hot grill according to the instructions given in Chapter 1.

2. Trim chicken breasts of all visible fat, and pound to an even thickness of ½ inch between 2 sheets of plastic wrap. Place chicken breasts in a mixing bowl.

3. To prepare dressing, bring a small saucepan of water to a boil over high heat. Add egg and boil for 1 minute. Remove egg from water with a slotted spoon and break it into a jar with a tight-fitting lid, scraping the inside of the shell. Add anchovy paste, garlic, lemon juice, and mustard, and shake well. Add ⅓ cup olive oil, and shake well again. Season to taste with pepper.

4. Reserve half of dressing, and mix remaining dressing into bowl with chicken breasts. Use reserved oil to brush both sides of bread.

5. Grill chicken for 2–3 minutes per side, uncovered, or until chicken is cooked through and no longer pink. Grill bread for 1–2 minutes per side, or until toasted. Remove chicken from the grill, and cut into thin slices against the grain. Remove bread from the grill, and cut into ½-inch croutons.

6. To serve, combine croutons, lettuce, and Parmesan in a mixing bowl, and toss with enough dressing to coat lightly. Mound mixture onto a serving platter or individual plates, and top with chicken slices. Serve immediately, passing extra dressing separately.

VARIATION: *Grilled shrimp or cubes of salmon can be used instead of chicken for an aquatic treat.*

Note: The dressing can be made up to 1 day in advance and refrigerated, tightly covered. Bring to room temperature before using.

Ingredients

- 1½ pounds boneless, skinless chicken breasts, rinsed and patted dry with paper towels
- 1 large egg
- 1 (2-ounce) tube anchovy paste
- 5 garlic cloves, minced
- ¼ cup freshly squeezed lemon juice
- 2 tablespoons Dijon mustard
- ½ cup extra-virgin olive oil, divided
- Freshly ground black pepper to taste
- 6–8 (½-inch-thick) slices French or Italian bread
- 6–8 cups bite-sized pieces baby greens or romaine lettuce, rinsed and dried
- ½ cup freshly grated Parmesan cheese
- 6–8 anchovy fillets (optional)

1 (2-pound) flank steak

⅓ cup rice wine vinegar

3 tablespoons soy sauce

3 tablespoons Dijon
mustard

2 tablespoons hoisin sauce*

3 tablespoons grated fresh
ginger

4 garlic cloves, peeled and
minced

2 scallions, trimmed and
finely chopped

Freshly ground black
pepper to taste

¾ cup vegetable oil

¼ cup Asian sesame oil*

¼ pound snow peas, tips
removed

1 pound baby spinach
leaves, rinsed and
stemmed

¼ pound bean sprouts,
rinsed

2 cucumbers, peeled,
halved, and thinly sliced

1 red bell pepper, seeds
and ribs removed, thinly
sliced

* Available in the Asian aisle
of most supermarkets and in
specialty markets.

Asian Steak Salad

Yield: 6–8 servings | Active time: 25 minutes | Start to finish: 4¼ hours, including 4 hours for marinating

1. Rinse steak and pat dry with paper towels. Score steak on both sides with a paring knife in a diagonal pattern ¼ inch deep.

2. Combine vinegar, soy sauce, mustard, hoisin sauce, ginger, garlic, scallions, and pepper in a jar with a tight-fitting lid. Shake well. Add vegetable and sesame oils and shake well again.

3. Place steak in a heavy resealable plastic bag, and add ½ cup of dressing. Marinate steak, refrigerated, for 4 hours, turning the bag occasionally.

4. While steak marinates, place snow peas in a microwave-safe container with 1 tablespoon water. Microwave on high (100%) for 30 seconds. Plunge snow peas into a bowl of ice water. Drain. Combine snow peas with spinach, bean sprouts, cucumbers, and red pepper in a salad bowl, and refrigerate.

5. Prepare a hot grill according to the instructions given in Chapter 1.

6. Grill steak for 5–7 minutes, uncovered if using a charcoal grill, or until browned. Turn meat with tongs, and grill for an additional 2–3 minutes for medium-rare, or to desired doneness. Allow steak to rest for 5 minutes, then slice it thinly on the diagonal.

7. To serve, toss salad with ⅓ cup of dressing. Mound mixture onto a serving platter or individual plates, and top with steak slices. Serve immediately, passing extra dressing separately.

VARIATION: *You can substitute slices of grilled chicken breast or fish steaks for the beef in this recipe. Consult a similar recipe for cooking instructions.*

Note: The dressing can be made up to 1 day in advance and refrigerated, tightly covered. Bring to room temperature before using.

Steak and Blue Cheese Salad

Yield: 4–6 servings | Active time: 25 minutes | Start to finish: 45 minutes

1. Prepare a dual-temperature hot-and-medium grill according to the instructions given in Chapter 1.

2. Sprinkle steaks with salt and pepper. Combine vinegar, garlic, shallot, parsley, thyme, sugar, salt, and pepper in a jar with a tight-fitting lid, and shake well. Add olive oil, and shake well again. Set aside.

3. Sear steaks on the hot side of the grill for 2–3 minutes per side, uncovered if using a charcoal grill, or until well browned. Transfer steaks to the cooler side of the grill, and cook for an additional 2–3 minutes per side for rare, when an instant-read thermometer registers 120°F. Remove steaks from the grill, and allow them to rest for 5 minutes.

4. Combine romaine, radicchio, onion, tomatoes, and blue cheese in a mixing bowl. To serve, toss salad with ⅓ cup of dressing. Mound mixture onto a serving platter or individual plates, and top with steak slices. Serve immediately, passing extra dressing separately.

Note: The dressing can be made up to 1 day in advance and refrigerated, tightly covered. Bring to room temperature before using.

1½ pounds New York strip steak or boneless rib eye steak, at least 1 inch thick

Salt and freshly ground black pepper to taste

½ cup red wine vinegar

2 garlic cloves, peeled and minced

1 shallot, peeled and minced

2 tablespoons chopped fresh parsley

1 tablespoon fresh thyme or 1 teaspoon dried

2 teaspoons granulated sugar

1 cup olive oil

4 cups bite-sized pieces romaine lettuce, rinsed and dried

1 large head radicchio, rinsed, cored, and chopped

½ small red onion, peeled and thinly sliced

½ pint cherry tomatoes, rinsed and halved

1 cup crumbled blue cheese

1 cup cracked-wheat bulgur

2 cups boiling water

1 (15-ounce) can garbanzo beans, drained and rinsed

2 large tomatoes, cored, seeded, and diced

1 cup chopped fresh parsley

1 bunch scallions, white parts and 2 inches of green tops, rinsed, trimmed, and thinly sliced

½ cup freshly squeezed lemon juice

¼ cup chopped fresh mint

¼ cup olive oil

Salt and freshly ground black pepper to taste

1 (3-pound) butterflied boneless leg of lamb (see method in Chapter 9)

3–4 (12-inch) metal skewers

½ head romaine lettuce, rinsed and dried

Middle Eastern Lamb Salad

Yield: 6–8 servings | Active time: 25 minutes | Start to finish: 1¼ hours

1. Place bulgur in a large mixing bowl. Stir in boiling water, cover the bowl, and allow bulgur to stand for 1 hour. Add beans, tomatoes, parsley, scallions, lemon juice, mint, olive oil, salt, and pepper to bulgur, and mix well. Refrigerate salad, tightly covered.

2. Prepare a hot grill according to the instructions given in Chapter 1. Preheat the oven to 375°F.

3. Sprinkle lamb with salt and pepper. Spear lamb lengthwise through the thickest part of the meat with the skewers to keep it level. Sear lamb on hot grill, uncovered, for 4 minutes per side.

4. Remove lamb from the grill, and place in a broiler pan. Roast lamb for 15–20 minutes, or until it registers 125°F for medium-rare on an instant-read thermometer. Remove lamb from the oven, and cover it loosely with foil. Allow lamb to rest for 10 minutes, then carve into slices across the grain.

5. To serve, line a platter or individual plates with lettuce leaves, and mound bulgur salad on top of lettuce. Top salad with lamb slices, and serve immediately.

Note: The lamb can be seared up to 4 hours in advance and kept at room temperature. The bulgur salad can be made up to 1 day in advance and refrigerated, tightly covered.

Pork Salad with Citrus Vinaigrette

Yield: 6–8 servings | Active time: 25 minutes | Start to finish: 50 minutes

1. Prepare a dual-temperature hot-and-medium grill according to the instructions given in Chapter 1.

2. Rinse pork and pat dry with paper towels. Sprinkle pork with salt and pepper. Combine chili powder, cumin, cinnamon, and allspice in a small bowl. Rub mixture over pork, and set aside.

3. Combine orange juice, lime juice, mustard, shallot, garlic, curry powder, thyme, salt, and pepper in a jar with a tight-fitting lid, and shake well. Add olive oil, and shake well again. Set aside.

4. Prepare oranges; first cut away peel and the white pith below it. Then, to separate orange segments from internal membranes, slice down to the core on either side of each segment; set segments aside as you go.

5. Grill pork, uncovered if using a charcoal grill, on the hot side of the grill for 2–3 minutes per side, turning it in quarter turns, and then move pork to the cooler side of the grill. Grill for an additional 5–6 minutes per side for medium. Allow pork to rest for 5 minutes, then slice pork on the diagonal into ½-inch slices.

6. Combine oranges, spinach, radicchio, red pepper, scallions, and avocados in a large mixing bowl. Toss salad with ⅓ cup dressing. Mound mixture onto a serving platter or individual plates, and top with pork slices. Serve immediately, passing extra dressing separately.

Note: The dressing can be made up to 1 day in advance and refrigerated, tightly covered. Bring to room temperature before using.

Ingredients

2 (¾-pound) pork tenderloins, trimmed of fat and silver skin (see method in Chapter 9)

Salt and freshly ground black pepper to taste

2 tablespoons chili powder

1 tablespoon ground cumin

1 teaspoon ground cinnamon

Pinch of ground allspice

¼ cup freshly squeezed orange juice

3 tablespoons freshly squeezed lime juice

1 tablespoon Dijon mustard

1 shallot, peeled and chopped

2 garlic cloves, peeled and minced

1 teaspoon curry powder

1 teaspoon fresh thyme or ¼ teaspoon dried

½ cup olive oil

3 navel oranges

¼ pound baby spinach, rinsed and dried

1 head radicchio, rinsed, cored, and shredded

1 red bell pepper, seeds and ribs removed, and thinly sliced

4 scallions, white parts and 2 inches of green tops, trimmed and thinly sliced

2 ripe avocados, stoned, peeled, and diced

1½ pounds thinly sliced
boneless pork chops

3 tablespoons freshly
squeezed orange juice

3 tablespoons freshly
squeezed lime juice

1 tablespoon sherry
vinegar

2 tablespoons chopped
fresh cilantro

2 garlic cloves, peeled and
minced

1 small serrano or jalapeño
chile, seeds and ribs
removed, and finely
chopped

Salt and freshly ground
black pepper to taste

½ cup extra-virgin olive oil

2 tablespoons chili powder

1 tablespoon ground cumin

2 red bell peppers, seeds
and ribs removed, and
quartered lengthwise

1 large red onion, peeled
and cut into ½-inch slices

4 cups bite-sized pieces
romaine lettuce, rinsed
and dried

2 large tomatoes, cored,
seeded, and diced

2 cups broken tortilla chips

Mexican Pork Salad

Yield: 4–6 servings | Active time: 20 minutes | Start to finish: 1 hour

1. Prepare a medium-hot grill according to the instructions given in Chapter 1. Rinse pork and pat dry with paper towels. Cut off all visible fat.

2. Combine orange juice, lime juice, vinegar, cilantro, garlic, chile, salt, and pepper in a jar with a tight-fitting lid, and shake well. Add olive oil, and shake well again. Pour half of dressing into a heavy resealable plastic bag, and add chili powder and cumin. Mix well. Add pork, and marinate at room temperature for 20 minutes, turning the bag occasionally.

3. Remove pork from marinade, and discard marinade. Grill pork for 3–4 minutes per side, or until cooked through. Brush vegetables with dressing. Grill pepper sections and onion slices for 4–5 minutes per side. Allow pork to rest for 5 minutes.

4. Cut peppers into strips, and separate onion slices into rings. Slice pork thinly against the grain.

5. Combine lettuce and tomato in a large mixing bowl. Toss salad with half of remaining dressing. Mound mixture onto a serving platter or individual plates, and top with pork, pepper, and onion slices. Sprinkle broken tortilla chips over all, and serve immediately, passing extra dressing separately.

VARIATION: *Boneless, skinless chicken breasts also work well in this recipe; consult a similar recipe for instructions on how to cook the chicken.*

Note: The dressing can be made up to 1 day in advance and refrigerated, tightly covered. Bring to room temperature before using.

Chapter 12

Combination Cooking

This chapter is not one you will find in many cookbooks on grilling; it is the result of literally decades of experimentation as I have tried to push the limits of what can be cooked on a grill and how to give food the best flavor. All of the recipes in this chapter start on the grill; they are then finished in a conventional oven. Some recipes are then roasted in a relatively cool oven to complete cooking, while others begin by being seared or smoked on the grill and are then braised to that wonderful term—fork tender.

Timing Rolled Roasts

Roasts cook more evenly if they are boned and rolled rather than left on the bone. While bones help retain moisture, the meat next to bones does not cook at the same rate since the bones act as insulation against the air carrying the heat. When tied, the string should be firm enough to hold the meat together in a neat cylinder, but should not be so tight as to be pressing into the flesh so that the exterior of the roast is bumpy. When the tissue is compressed at the points where the strings are tied, those portions of meat will cook at a slower rate, so the interior will not be evenly cooked.

Here is a chart of the general temperatures to which meats are roasted:

Roasting Temperatures for Meat	
MEAT	**DESIRED INTERNAL TEMPERATURE**
Beef and Lamb	120°F—Rare 125°F–130°F—Medium-Rare 135°F—Medium
Pork	145°F–150°F
Veal	150°F–155°F

While most cookbooks calculate roasting times in an equation of minutes per pound, I have a different method. I roast meats by the circumference. A 3-pound boneless pork loin can be short and squat, or it can be long and thin.

The easiest way to determine the circumference of a roast is with a tape measure. Stand the roast on its end, and place the tape measure snugly around what

87

would be the waistline. Here is a chart to help you judge when to start taking the temperature of different roasts.

ROASTING TIMES FOR MEATS

These are total times for boneless roasts, with the initial searing taking place on the grill, and then the meat roasted in a 350°F oven for the remainder of the cooking time.

Roasting Times for Meats			
CIRCUMFERENCE	BEEF/LAMB (125°F)	VEAL (150°F)	PORK (150°F)
9 inches	30–35 min.	50–55 min.	55–60 min.
10 inches	35–45 min.	55–65 min.	60–70 min.
11 inches	45–50 min.	65–70 min.	75–85 min.
12 inches	55–60 min.	70–75 min.	85–95 min.
13 inches	60–65 min.	75–85 min.	95–105 min.
14 inches	70–75 min.	85–95 min.	105–115 min.
15 inches	75–80 min.	95–110 min.	115–125 min.
16 inches	80–90 min.	110–115 min.	125–130 min.

Leg of Lamb with Garlic, Rosemary, and Lemon
Yield: 6–8 servings | Active time: 20 minutes | Start to finish: 1½ hours

½ leg of lamb, boned, rolled, and tied, to yield 3 pounds meat

1 cup mesquite chips

10 garlic cloves, peeled

Zest of 1 lemon, cut into thin strips

3 sprigs fresh rosemary, leaves removed

1 tablespoon kosher salt

1 teaspoon freshly ground black pepper

½ cup beef stock

1. Allow meat to reach room temperature, and cut deep slits into any thick portions with a paring knife.

2. Prepare a hot grill according to the instructions given in Chapter 1. If using a charcoal grill, soak mesquite chips in water for 30 minutes. If using a gas grill, create a packet for wood chips as described in Chapter 1.

3. Combine garlic, lemon zest, and rosemary leaves in a food processor fitted with a steel blade and chop finely, using on-and-off pulsing. Scrape mixture into a small bowl and stir in salt and pepper. Stuff garlic mixture into all the crevices of the meat formed when it was boned, as well as into the slits. Rub some of mixture all over exterior of roast.

4. Preheat the oven to 350°F. Place mesquite chips on the grill. Sear lamb for a total of 10 minutes, covered, turning with tongs to sear all sides. Remove lamb from the grill and place in a roasting pan.

5. Roast lamb, uncovered, for 45–60 minutes, or until the temperature registers 125°F on an instant-read thermometer. The roasting time will depend on the thickness of the roll; consult the chart at the beginning of this chapter. Remove lamb from the oven, place it on a platter, and loosely cover with aluminum foil. Allow lamb to rest for 15 minutes, to allow juices to be reabsorbed into meat.

6. Pour grease out of the roasting pan and pour in stock. Place the pan over medium-high heat and stir often to dislodge any brown bits clinging to the bottom of the pan. Carve the meat into slices, adding any juices to the pan, and pass sauce separately.

Note: The roast can be seared up to 3 hours in advance of roasting it; keep it at room temperature, lightly covered.

Pork Loin with Smoked Apple Chutney

Yield: 6–8 servings | Active time: 25 minutes | Start to finish: 1¾ hours

1. Prepare a hot grill according to the instructions given in Chapter 1. If using a charcoal grill, soak hickory or apple wood chips in water for 30 minutes. If using a gas grill, create a packet for wood chips as described in Chapter 1.

2. Rinse pork and pat dry with paper towels. Combine 3 garlic cloves, sage, thyme, allspice, salt, and pepper in a small bowl. Rub mixture into surfaces of pork.

3. Preheat the oven to 350°F. Place wood chips on the grill. Sear pork for a total of 10 minutes, covered, turning with tongs to sear all sides. Remove pork from the grill and place in a roasting pan.

4. Roast pork, uncovered, for 45–60 minutes, or until the temperature registers 145°F on an instant-read thermometer. The roasting time will depend on the thickness of the meat; consult the chart at the beginning of this chapter.

5. While pork roasts, prepare chutney. Cover the grill with a small-holed fish grill and place tomatoes, onion, and apple on the grill. Cover the grill with a lid and smoke vegetables and apple for 10 minutes. Remove vegetables and apple from the grill. Peel, core, and seed tomatoes. Peel and finely dice onion, and apples. Place them in a large saucepan and add remaining garlic, sugar, vinegar, raisins, ginger, and cayenne.

6. Bring chutney to a boil over medium heat. Simmer, uncovered, for 30 minutes, or until thick, stirring occasionally.

7. Remove pork from the oven and place it on a platter loosely covered with aluminum foil. Allow pork to rest for 15 minutes to allow juices to be reabsorbed into meat. Then slice thinly against the grain. Serve immediately, and pass chutney separately.

Note: The roast can be seared up to 3 hours in advance of roasting it; keep it at room temperature, lightly covered.

2 cups hickory or apple wood chips

1 (3-pound) boneless center cut pork loin roast

5 garlic cloves, peeled and minced, divided

2 tablespoons dried sage

1 tablespoon dried thyme

½ teaspoon ground allspice

Salt and freshly ground black pepper to taste

3 large tomatoes, cut in half

1 large onion, cut in half

1 Granny Smith apple, peeled, cored, and quartered

½ cup granulated sugar

½ cup cider vinegar

¼ cup golden raisins

2 tablespoons grated fresh ginger

¼ teaspoon cayenne

1 cup mesquite, hickory, or apple wood chips

1 (3½–4-pound) whole chicken, giblets removed

4 sprigs fresh parsley, divided

4 sprigs fresh rosemary, divided

6 garlic cloves, peeled, divided

1 orange, quartered

Salt and freshly ground black pepper to taste

4 tablespoons (½ stick) unsalted butter, softened

1 small onion, peeled and roughly chopped

1 carrot, peeled and thickly sliced

1 celery rib, rinsed, trimmed, and roughly chopped

1½ cups chicken stock, divided

Aromatic Roast Chicken

Serves: 4 | Active time: 15 minutes | Start to finish: 2 hours

1. Prepare a medium-hot grill according to the instructions given in Chapter 1. If using a charcoal grill, soak wood chips in water for 30 minutes. If using a gas grill, create a packet for wood chips as described in Chapter 1.

2. Rinse chicken, and pat dry with paper towels. Place 2 sprigs each of parsley and rosemary, 3 garlic cloves, and orange quarters in cavity of chicken. Sprinkle salt and pepper inside cavity, and close cavity with skewers.

3. Chop remaining parsley, rosemary, and garlic, and mix with butter. Season to taste with salt and pepper. Gently stuff mixture under skin of breast meat. Rub skin with salt and pepper. Truss chicken, if desired.

4. Preheat the oven to 350°F. Place wood chips on the grill. Sear chicken for a total of 15 minutes, covered, turning with tongs to brown all sides. Remove chicken from the grill, and place in a roasting pan, breast-side up.

5. Add onion, carrot, celery, and ½ cup chicken stock to the roasting pan. Cook an additional 1–1¼ hours, or until the juices run clear and the temperature of the dark meat registers 180°F on an instant-read thermometer. Remove chicken from the oven, and allow it to rest for 10 minutes, lightly covered.

6. Spoon all grease out of the pan, and add remaining chicken stock to the pan. Stir over medium-high heat until liquid is reduced to a syrupy consistency. Strain sauce into a sauce boat, and add to it any liquid that accumulates on the platter when chicken is carved. Carve chicken, and serve immediately.

VARIATION: *Tarragon can be substituted for the rosemary and parsley, and white wine can be used instead of chicken stock.*

Note: The chicken can be prepared for searing and roasting up to 6 hours in advance and refrigerated, tightly covered.

Aromatic Roast Chicken

Smoked Beef Brisket with Barbecue Sauce

Yield: 8–10 servings | Active time: 20 minutes | Start to finish: 3½ hours

1. Prepare a medium-hot grill according to the instructions given in Chapter 1. If using a charcoal grill, soak hickory or mesquite chips in water for 30 minutes. If using a gas grill, create a packet for wood chips as described in Chapter 1.

2. Rinse brisket and pat dry with paper towels. Rub brisket with garlic, and season to taste with salt and pepper.

3. Preheat the oven to 350°F. Place wood chips on the grill. Sear brisket, covered, for a total of 20 minutes, turning with tongs after 10 minutes.

4. Transfer brisket to a roasting pan, and add stock. Bring to a boil on top of the stove, then transfer to the oven, and bake for 2–2½ hours, covered, or until fork tender.

5. Remove brisket to a warm platter and tip the roasting pan to spoon off as much grease as possible. Slice brisket against the grain into thin slices. Spoon some pan juices over meat, and pass barbecue sauce separately.

VARIATION: *You can also use this recipe for a boneless pork shoulder; the cooking time will be reduced to 1½–2 hours.*

Note: The brisket can be prepared up to 2 days in advance and refrigerated. If cooked in advance, remove the layer of grease, which will have hardened on the top. Reheat, covered, in a 350°F oven for 25–35 minutes, or until hot.

2 cups hickory or mesquite chips

1 (3–4-pound) beef brisket

2 garlic cloves, peeled and crushed

Salt and freshly ground black pepper to taste

2 cups beef stock

1 cup My Favorite Barbecue Sauce (recipe on page 16) or commercial barbecue sauce, heated

1 cup mesquite chips

6 (1-pound) lamb shanks

Salt and freshly ground
   black pepper to taste

⅓ cup olive oil

2 medium onions, peeled
   and diced

2 celery ribs, rinsed,
   trimmed, and diced

2 carrots, peeled, trimmed,
   and sliced

4 garlic cloves, peeled and
   minced

2 tablespoons chopped
   fresh parsley

1 tablespoon chopped
   fresh rosemary or 1
   teaspoon dried

1 tablespoon chopped
   fresh oregano or 1
   teaspoon dried

2 teaspoons fresh thyme or
   ½ teaspoon dried

2 tablespoons tomato
   paste

½ cups Barolo, or other dry
   red wine

1 cup beef stock

1 tablespoon cornstarch

2 tablespoons cold water

Braised Lamb Shanks

Yield: 6 servings | Active time: 20 minutes | Start to finish: 3 hours

1. Prepare a medium-hot grill according to the instructions given in Chapter 1. If using a charcoal grill, soak mesquite chips in water for 30 minutes. If using a gas grill, create a packet for wood chips as described in Chapter 1.

2. Wipe lamb shanks well with a damp cloth and remove any fat. Season with salt and pepper, and set aside.

3. While grill heats, heat oil in a Dutch oven over medium-high heat. Add onions, celery, carrots, and garlic, and cook, stirring frequently, for 3 minutes, or until onions are translucent.

4. Preheat the oven to 350°F. Place mesquite chips on the grill. Sear lamb shanks for a total of 15 minutes, covered, turning shanks with tongs to sear all sides.

5. Transfer shanks to the Dutch oven, and add parsley, rosemary, oregano, thyme, tomato paste, wine, and stock. Bring to a boil on top of the stove, then transfer to the oven, and bake for 1½–2 hours, or until fork tender.

6. Remove shanks to a warm platter and tip the Dutch oven to spoon off as much grease as possible. Cook sauce over medium heat until reduced by half. Mix cornstarch and water in a small cup, and add to sauce. Simmer for 3 minutes or until lightly thickened. Season sauce to taste with salt and pepper, then pour sauce over shanks, and serve immediately.

Note: The shanks can be prepared up to 3 days in advance and refrigerated. If cooked in advance, remove the layer of grease, which will have hardened on the top. Reheat, covered, in a 350°F oven for 25–35 minutes, or until hot.

Braised Lamb Shanks

Chapter 13

Pizzas

Cooking thin-crust pizzas on the grill is now all the rage, and they can be topped with myriad ingredients. The key to a successful grilled pizza is that they must be small; it is impossible to flip a large round on the grill, and it is essential to grill both sides of the dough. I usually make pizzas in two batches, and cut up the first batch to allow diners to start munching while the second batch cooks. If your grill is large enough to accommodate all four circles at once, go ahead and cook them simultaneously.

For an easy alternative to making pizza dough, in almost all cities you can now purchase ready-to-bake balls of pizza dough in the refrigerated dairy case. With a few balls of pizza dough handy, any pizza can be on the table in less time than it takes to have one delivered!

Basic Pizza Dough and Procedure

Yield: 4 (8-inch) pizzas | Active time: 15 minutes | Start to finish: 50 minutes, including 30 minutes for rising

3 cups all-purpose flour, plus extra for working dough

1 package active dry or fresh yeast

1 teaspoon salt

1 tablespoon honey

2 tablespoons olive oil

¾ cup water

1. Place flour and yeast in a mixing bowl or the bowl of an electric mixer fitted with a dough hook. Add salt, honey, olive oil, and water. Mix well until the dough forms a soft ball.

2. Transfer dough to a lightly floured surface and knead for 5 minutes or until smooth. Place dough in a greased deep mixing bowl and allow dough to rest, covered with a clean dry towel, for 30 minutes.

3. Divide dough into 4 equal parts, and roll each piece into a smooth, tight ball. Place balls on a flat dish, covered with a damp towel, and refrigerate until grilling time. (This can be done up to 6 hours in advance, but dough should be removed from the refrigerator 1 hour before grilling to reach room temperature.)

4. Lightly flour a work surface, and using the fleshy part of your fingertips, flatten each dough ball into a circle approximately 6 inches in diameter, leaving outer edge thicker than center. Dust dough on both sides with flour. Lift dough from the work surface and gently stretch the edges, working clockwise, to form dough circles that are ¼ inch thick. Sprinkle additional flour on pizza paddles or baking sheets, and place pizza circles on top of flour. Lightly rub a long sheet of plastic wrap with flour, then invert loosely over pizza rounds and let them stand to puff slightly while preparing the grill, 10 to 20 minutes.

VARIATIONS: *Feel free to add a few tablespoons of chopped fresh herbs to the basic pizza dough.*

---

1 recipe Basic Pizza Dough or purchased pizza dough

½ pound fresh chorizo sausage, casings removed if necessary

1 cup firmly packed arugula leaves, rinsed and dried

10 ounces soft fresh goat cheese, crumbled

Salt and freshly ground black pepper to taste

3 tablespoons olive oil

2 garlic cloves, peeled and pushed through a garlic press

¼ red bell pepper, seeds and ribs removed, and chopped

¼ orange bell pepper, seeds and ribs removed, and chopped

2 (10-inch) aluminum pie tins

Chorizo and Goat Cheese Pizza

Yield: 4 servings | Active time: 25 minutes | Start to finish: 50 minutes

1. Prepare a medium-hot grill according to the instructions given in Chapter 1. Shape pizza dough into 4 individual ¼-inch-thick rounds as described above in the recipe for Basic Pizza Dough.

2. Place chorizo in a skillet over medium-high heat, and cook, breaking up lumps with a fork, for 5–7 minutes, or until sausage is browned. Remove sausage from the pan with a slotted spoon, and drain on paper towels. Combine arugula and goat cheese in a small bowl, and season to taste with salt and pepper. Combine olive oil and garlic in a small bowl, and stir well.

3. Brush dough rounds with seasoned olive oil. Gently flip 2 dough rounds onto the grill, oiled-side down. Grill, uncovered, for 1½–2 minutes, or until grill marks form; burst bubbles that may appear on the surface with a long-handled meat fork. Brush tops with olive oil, and invert pizzas onto a baking sheet with the grilled side up.

4. Spread cheese mixture on pizzas, leaving a ½-inch margin. Top with chorizo and peppers.

5. Return pizzas to the grill, and cover with pie tins. Grill, covered, for 1½–2 minutes, or until browned and cheese has melted. Serve immediately, and repeat with remaining 2 pizza rounds.

Pizza Margherita

Yield: 4 servings | Active time: 20 minutes | Start to finish: 30 minutes

1. Prepare a medium-hot grill according to the instructions given in Chapter 1. Shape pizza dough into 4 individual ¼-inch-thick rounds as described above in the recipe for Basic Pizza Dough.

2. Place tomatoes in a sieve set over a mixing bowl to drain. Brush dough rounds with olive oil, and sprinkle with salt and pepper. Gently flip 2 dough rounds onto the grill, oiled-side down. Grill, uncovered, for 1½–2 minutes, or until grill marks form; burst bubbles that may appear on the surface with a long-handled meat fork. Brush tops with olive oil, and invert pizzas onto a baking sheet with the grilled side up.

3. Cover crusts with mozzarella and then tomatoes, stopping ½ inch from the edge. Scatter basil and Parmesan over the top. Season to taste with salt and pepper, and drizzle with more olive oil.

4. Return pizzas to the grill, and cover with pie tins. Grill, covered, for 1½–2 minutes, or until browned and cheese has melted. Serve immediately, and repeat with remaining 2 pizza rounds.

VARIATION: *While it would not be authentic, either fresh oregano or fresh chopped rosemary can be substituted for the basil.*

1 recipe Basic Pizza Dough or purchased pizza dough

8 ripe plum tomatoes, rinsed, cored, seeded, and chopped

¼ cup extra-virgin olive oil, divided

Salt and freshly ground black pepper to taste

½ pound whole-milk mozzarella cheese, thinly sliced

½ cup firmly packed fresh basil leaves

¼ cup freshly grated Parmesan cheese

2 (10-inch) aluminum pie tins

Pizza Margherita

Provençal Vegetable Pizza

1 recipe Basic Pizza Dough, or purchased pizza dough

2 medium yellow squash, trimmed and cut into ¼-inch slices

2 Italian eggplant, trimmed and cut into ¼-inch slices

1 red bell pepper, seeds and ribs removed, and quartered lengthwise

½ cup extra-virgin olive oil, divided

Salt and freshly ground black pepper to taste

¾ cup black olive tapenade, homemade or purchased

3 tablespoons chopped fresh oregano, or 1 tablespoon dried

2 tablespoons chopped fresh parsley

1 tablespoon fresh thyme or 1 teaspoon dried

2 cups grated Gruyère cheese

2 (10-inch) aluminum pie tins

Provençal Vegetable Pizza

Yield: 4 servings | Active time: 20 minutes | Start to finish: 35 minutes

1. Prepare a medium-hot grill according to the instructions given in Chapter 1. Shape pizza dough into 4 individual ¼-inch-thick rounds as described above in the recipe for Basic Pizza Dough.

2. Brush squash, eggplant, and pepper slices with olive oil, and sprinkle with salt and pepper. Grill squash and eggplant for 2 minutes per side, covered, or until tender. Grill pepper slices for 5 minutes per side, covered, or until tender. When cool enough to handle, slice peppers into thin strips. Combine tapenade, oregano, parsley, and thyme in a small bowl, and stir well. Set aside.

3. Brush dough rounds with olive oil, and sprinkle with salt and pepper. Gently flip 2 dough rounds onto the grill, oiled side down. Grill, uncovered, for 1½–2 minutes, or until grill marks form; burst bubbles that may appear on the surface with a long-handled meat fork. Brush tops with olive oil, and invert pizzas onto a baking sheet with the grilled side up.

4. Spread crusts with tapenade mixture, stopping ½ inch from the edge. Divide one quarter of vegetables on top of tapenade, and then sprinkle with ½ cup cheese.

5. Return pizzas to the grill, and cover with pie tins. Grill, covered, for 1½–2 minutes, or until browned and cheese has melted. Serve immediately, and repeat with remaining 2 pizza rounds.

Note: The vegetables can be grilled up to 1 day in advance and refrigerated, tightly covered. Allow them to reach room temperature before using.

Bacon, Tomato, Mushroom, and Cheddar Pizza

Yield: 4 servings | Active time: 15 minutes | Start to finish: 35 minutes

1. Prepare a medium-hot grill according to the instructions given in Chapter 1. Shape pizza dough into 4 individual ¼-inch-thick rounds as described above in the recipe for Basic Pizza Dough.

2. Place bacon slices in a heavy skillet, and cook over medium-high heat, turning pieces as necessary, until bacon is crisp. Remove bacon with tongs, and drain on paper towels. When cool, crumble bacon, and set aside.

3. Brush dough rounds with olive oil, and sprinkle with salt and pepper. Gently flip 2 dough rounds onto the grill, oiled-side down. Grill, uncovered, for 1½–2 minutes, or until grill marks form; burst bubbles that may appear on the surface with a long-handled meat fork. Brush tops with olive oil, and invert pizzas onto a baking sheet with the grilled side up.

4. Cover crusts with cheddar, then tomatoes and mushrooms, stopping ½ inch from the edge. Scatter bacon over the top. Season to taste with salt and pepper.

5. Return pizzas to the grill, and cover with pie tins. Grill, covered, for 1½–2 minutes, or until browned and cheese has melted. Serve immediately, and repeat with remaining 2 pizza rounds.

1 recipe Basic Pizza Dough or purchased pizza dough

¼ pound smoked bacon

¼ cup extra-virgin olive oil

Salt and freshly ground pepper to taste

3 cups grated cheddar cheese

4 ripe plum tomatoes, rinsed, cored, seeded, and thinly sliced

1 cup sliced mushrooms

2 (10-inch) aluminum pie tins

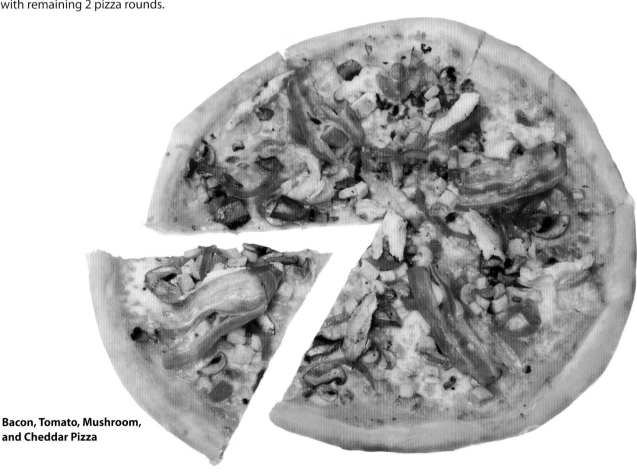

Bacon, Tomato, Mushroom, and Cheddar Pizza

4 ripe plum tomatoes, rinsed, cored, seeded, and diced

½ cup chopped pitted kalamata olives

¼ cup chopped red onion

4 tablespoons olive oil, divided

2 tablespoons chopped fresh oregano or 2 teaspoons dried

Salt and freshly ground black pepper to taste

4 (8-inch) whole-wheat pita breads

½ cup crumbled feta cheese

2 (10-inch) aluminum pie tins

Greek-Style Pita Pizzas

Yield: 4 servings | Active time: 10 minutes | Start to finish: 35 minutes

1. Prepare a medium-hot grill according to the instructions given in Chapter 1. Combine tomatoes, olives, onion, 2 tablespoons olive oil, oregano, salt, and pepper in a mixing bowl. Mix well.

2. Brush pita breads with olive oil, and sprinkle with salt and pepper. Gently flip 2 pita breads onto the grill, oiled-side down. Grill, uncovered, for 1½–2 minutes, or until grill marks form. Brush tops with olive oil, and invert pitas onto a baking sheet with the grilled side up.

3. Cover crusts with vegetable mixture, stopping ½ inch from the edge. Scatter feta over the top. Season to taste with salt and pepper.

4. Return pizzas to the grill, and cover with pie tins. Grill, covered, for 1½–2 minutes, or until browned and cheese has melted. Serve immediately.

Chapter 14

Vegetables

It is only in recent decades that Americans have come to appreciate the wonderful flavors and textures that result from grilling vegetables. Cooking vegetables over high heat evaporates some of the high water content, and, therefore, intensifies the natural, sweet flavor.

Grilling accentuates vegetables' natural sugars.

8–12 (8-inch) bamboo skewers

¼ cup olive oil

3 garlic cloves, peeled and minced

1 red onion, peeled

2 orange or yellow bell peppers, seeds and ribs removed, and halved

1 Italian eggplant

2 small zucchini, trimmed

2 portobello mushroom caps, stemmed, and wiped with a damp paper towel

Salt and freshly ground black pepper to taste

Mixed Vegetable Kebabs

Yield: 4–6 servings | Active time: 20 minutes | Start to finish: 45 minutes

1. Soak bamboo skewers in warm water to cover, and prepare a medium-hot grill according to the instructions given in Chapter 1.

2. Mix garlic with oil, and set aside. Cut onion in half horizontally, and then cut halves into 8 wedges each. Cut bell peppers into 1½-inch squares. Cut eggplant into 1½-inch cubes. Cut zucchini into 1½-inch segments. Cut mushroom caps into eighths.

3. Rub all vegetables with garlic oil, and sprinkle with salt and pepper.

4. Thread vegetables alternately onto 2 parallel skewers. Grill kebabs, covered, giving them quarter turns every 2½–3 minutes, for a total of 10–12 minutes, or until vegetables are tender. Remove kebabs from the grill, and serve immediately.

Note: The kebabs can be prepared for grilling up to 6 hours in advance and kept at room temperature.

10 (8-inch) bamboo skewers

2 pounds medium asparagus

3 tablespoons olive oil

Salt and freshly ground black pepper to taste

Grilled Asparagus

Yield: 4–6 servings | Active time: 10 minutes | Start to finish: 30 minutes

1. Soak bamboo skewers in warm water to cover, and prepare a medium-hot grill according to the instructions given in Chapter 1.

2. Break off woody ends from asparagus, soak asparagus in water to cover for 10 minutes, and rub the tips to dislodge any lingering grit.

3. Divide asparagus into groups, and thread them horizontally with 2 skewers per bunch into loose groups; do not push them together too tightly. Brush asparagus with oil, and sprinkle with salt and pepper.

4. Grill asparagus, covered, for 3–4 minutes per side, turning bunches with tongs. Serve immediately.

Garlicky Artichokes

Yield: 4–6 servings | Active time: 20 minutes | Start to finish: 1 hour

2 tablespoons freshly squeezed lemon juice

4 large globe artichokes

¼ cup olive oil

4 garlic cloves, peeled and minced, divided

Salt and freshly ground black pepper to taste

4 tablespoons unsalted butter, melted

1. Fill a large mixing bowl with cold water, and add lemon juice. Cut off stem and top 1 inch from 1 artichoke. Bend back dark green outer leaves until they break off, and discard. Cut artichoke lengthwise into quarters, and place in acidulated water. Repeat with remaining artichokes.

2. Prepare a vegetable steamer, and steam artichokes for 25–30 minutes, or until tender when the heart is pierced with the tip of a paring knife. When artichokes are cool enough to handle, remove the hairy choke and small purple-tipped leaves from the center of each quarter.

3. Prepare a medium-hot grill according to the instructions given in Chapter 1.

4. Combine oil and 1 garlic clove, rub mixture on artichokes, and sprinkle artichokes with salt and pepper. Mix remaining garlic and butter, season with salt and pepper, and set aside.

5. Grill artichokes for a total of 8–9 minutes, uncovered if using a charcoal grill, turning them gently with tongs, or until grill marks appear. Remove artichokes from the grill and drizzle with garlic butter. Serve immediately.

Note: The artichokes can be steamed up to 1 day in advance and refrigerated, tightly covered.

Garlicky Artichokes

4–6 ears fresh corn

Kitchen twine

3 tablespoons unsalted
butter, melted

Salt and freshly ground
black pepper to taste

Grilled Corn

Yield: 4–6 servings | Active time: 10 minutes | Start to finish: 35 minutes

1. Prepare a medium-hot grill according to the instructions given in Chapter 1.

2. Break stem end off corn, and discard all but 1 layer of husks. Pull back remaining husks, and pull off as much corn silk as possible. Draw husks back over kernels, and tie husks with kitchen twine. Soak corn in cold water to cover for 10 minutes.

3. Grill corn, uncovered if using a charcoal grill, for a total of 8–10 minutes, turning it with tongs every 1½–2 minutes. Corn is done when husks are charred and outline of kernels is visible.

4. Remove corn from the grill, and when cool enough to handle, remove and discard husks and any remaining corn silks. To serve, brush corn with melted butter, and season with salt and pepper to taste. Serve immediately.

Grilled Corn

Rosemary Potatoes

Yield: 4–6 servings | Active time: 20 minutes | Start to finish: 1 hour

1. Soak bamboo skewers in warm water to cover, and prepare a medium-hot grill according to the instructions given in Chapter 1.

2. Place potatoes in a saucepan, and cover with cold water. Salt water, and bring potatoes to a boil over high heat. Reduce the heat to medium-high, and boil potatoes for 10–12 minutes, or until just tender. Drain potatoes, and toss them with ¼ cup olive oil, rosemary, salt, and pepper.

3. Thread potatoes onto 2 parallel skewers. Grill potatoes, uncovered if using a charcoal grill, for a total of 4–5 minutes, turning them with tongs occasionally, or until grill marks appear. Remove skewers from the grill, and drizzle with remaining olive oil. Serve immediately.

VARIATION: *In place of rosemary, try fresh oregano or basil in this recipe, and you can add a few crushed garlic cloves to the oil too.*

- 8–12 (8-inch) bamboo skewers
- 1½ pounds baby potatoes, no more than 2 inches in diameter, scrubbed and halved
- Salt and freshly ground black pepper to taste
- ⅓ cup olive oil, divided
- 3 tablespoons finely chopped fresh rosemary

Herbed Zucchini

Yield: 4–6 servings | Active time: 15 minutes | Start to finish: 35 minutes

1. Prepare a medium-hot grill according to the instructions given in Chapter 1.

2. Cut zucchini in half lengthwise. Cut a thin slice off the curved side of each half with a paring knife so that zucchini sit securely on the counter. Combine oil, oregano, parsley, thyme, garlic, salt, and pepper in a blender. Puree until smooth, and scrape mixture into a small bowl.

3. Brush both sides of zucchini halves with oil mixture , and grill for 4–5 minutes per side, uncovered if using a charcoal grill, turning slices with tongs. Serve immediately or at room temperature.

Note: Both the zucchini and the oil mixture can be prepared up to 6 hours in advance and refrigerated separately, tightly covered.

- 4–6 small zucchini, rinsed and trimmed
- ⅓ cup extra-virgin olive oil
- 2 tablespoons fresh oregano or 2 teaspoons dried
- ¼ cup firmly packed fresh parsley leaves
- 2 teaspoons fresh thyme or ½ teaspoon dried
- 1 garlic clove, peeled
- Salt and freshly ground black pepper to taste

4 medium ripe tomatoes

2 tablespoons extra-virgin olive oil

1 garlic clove, peeled and pressed through a garlic press

1 teaspoon dried oregano

1 teaspoon dried thyme

Salt and freshly ground black pepper

⅔ cup Greek Feta Sauce (recipe on page 18)

Herbed Tomatoes with Greek Feta Sauce

Yield: 4 servings | Active time: 10 minutes | Start to finish: 35 minutes

1. Prepare a medium-hot grill according to the instructions given in Chapter 1. Cut tomatoes in half, and squeeze gently to remove seeds.

2. Combine oil, garlic, oregano, thyme, salt, and pepper in a small bowl, and stir well. Brush mixture on both sides of tomato halves.

3. Grill tomatoes skin-side up, uncovered if using a charcoal grill, for 3–4 minutes, or until grill marks show. Turn tomatoes gently with tongs and grill for an additional 2–3 minutes, or until hot. Serve immediately, passing Greek Feta Sauce separately.

Herbed Tomatoes with Greek Feta Sauce

Sesame Radicchio

Yield: 4–6 servings | Active time: 20 minutes | Start to finish: 45 minutes

1. Prepare a medium-hot grill according to the instructions given in Chapter 1.

2. Trim root end from radicchio, and cut each head into quarters, leaving core attached. Brush radicchio and scallions with 2 tablespoons sesame oil, and sprinkle with salt and pepper. Set aside.

3. Combine vinegar, soy sauce, sherry, garlic, ginger, and pepper in a jar with a tight-fitting lid, and shake well. Add remaining sesame oil and vegetable oil, and shake well again. Set aside.

4. Grill radicchio for 3 minutes per side, covered, turning wedges with tongs. Grill scallions for a total of 4 minutes, turning them once. Remove vegetables from the grill.

5. Cut core from radicchio wedges, and cut each wedge crosswise into ½-inch strips. Cut scallions into thirds. Transfer vegetables to a mixing bowl, and toss with dressing. Sprinkle with sesame seeds, and serve immediately.

Note: The dressing can be prepared up to 1 day in advance and refrigerated, tightly covered. Allow it to reach room temperature before using.

3 (4-inch) heads radicchio

12 scallions, white parts and 1 inch of green tops only, rinsed and trimmed

¼ cup Asian sesame oil, divided*

Salt and freshly ground black pepper to taste

¼ cup rice wine vinegar

2 tablespoons soy sauce

1 tablespoon mirin* or sherry

2 garlic cloves, peeled and minced

2 teaspoons grated fresh ginger

¼ cup vegetable oil

3 tablespoons sesame seeds, toasted

* Available in the Asian aisle of most supermarkets and in specialty markets.

Chapter 15

Non-Grilled Side Dishes

While there are recipes for vegetable and other side dishes in this book that are cooked on the grill, there are many times that the grill is reserved for the entree, and the supporting players are created in the kitchen. You will find those recipes in this chapter.

½ cup sugar

½ cup cider vinegar

⅓ cup vegetable oil

1 tablespoon celery seeds

1 tablespoon dry mustard

Salt and freshly ground black pepper to taste

1 (2-pound) head green cabbage, cored and shredded

1 small red onion, peeled and thinly sliced

1 green pepper, seeds and ribs removed, and thinly sliced

1 red bell pepper, seeds and ribs removed, and thinly sliced

Celery Seed Slaw

Yield: 6–8 servings | Active time: 20 minutes | Start to finish: 6¼ hours, including 5 hours to marinate and chill

1. Combine sugar, vinegar, and oil in a small saucepan, and bring to a boil over medium heat, stirring occasionally. Reduce the heat to low and stir in celery seeds, mustard, salt, and pepper. Simmer for 2 minutes, stirring occasionally.

2. Combine cabbage, onion, green pepper, and red pepper in a large mixing bowl. Toss dressing with slaw. Allow slaw to sit at room temperature for 2 hours, tossing it occasionally. Refrigerate slaw for 3–4 hours. Drain well before serving.

Note: The slaw can be made 1 day in advance and refrigerated, tightly covered with plastic wrap.

---

3 cucumbers, peeled, halved lengthwise, seeded, and thinly sliced

½ large sweet onion such as Vidalia or Bermuda, peeled and thinly sliced

1 cup rice wine vinegar

3 tablespoons chopped fresh dill

2 tablespoons granulated sugar

Salt and freshly ground white pepper to taste

Dilled Cucumbers

Yield: 6–8 servings | Active time: 10 minutes | Start to finish: 2 hours 10 minutes, including 2 hours for marinating

1. Combine cucumbers and onion in a heavy resealable plastic bag. Combine vinegar, dill, sugar, salt, and pepper in a jar with a tight-fitting lid. Shake well to dissolve sugar.

2. Add cucumbers, and marinate for at least 2 hours, refrigerated, turning the bag occasionally. Drain marinade from salad. Serve chilled.

Note: The salad can be made up to 2 days in advance and refrigerated, tightly covered.

Jicama Slaw

Yield: 4–6 servings | Active time: 20 minutes | Start to finish: 35 minutes

1. Combine jicama, red pepper, orange pepper, and onion in a mixing bowl. Combine lime juice, cilantro, oil, salt, and pepper in a jar with a tight-fitting lid, and shake well.

2. Pour dressing over vegetables, and toss to combine. Allow slaw to sit for at least 15 minutes for flavors to blend.

Note: The slaw can be made up to 1 day in advance and refrigerated, tightly covered. Allow it to reach room temperature before serving.

1 medium jicama, peeled and cut into matchstick strips

1 red bell pepper, seeds and ribs removed, and cut into matchstick strips

1 orange bell pepper, seeds and ribs removed, and cut into matchstick strips

½ small red onion, peeled and cut into matchstick strips

3 tablespoons freshly squeezed lime juice

3 tablespoons chopped fresh cilantro

2 tablespoons olive oil

Salt and freshly ground black pepper to taste

Pico de Gallo

Yield: 2 cups | Active time: 15 minutes | Start to finish: 30 minutes

Combine tomatoes, onion, garlic, cilantro, chile, lime juice, olive oil, salt, and pepper in a mixing bowl, and stir well. Allow mixture to sit at room temperature for 15 minutes so that flavors will blend.

Note: The relish can be prepared up to 6 hours in advance and kept at room temperature; drain off excess liquid before serving.

4 large ripe tomatoes, rinsed, cored, seeded, and chopped

½ medium red onion, peeled and chopped

3 garlic cloves, peeled and minced

¼ cup chopped fresh cilantro

1 jalapeño or serrano chile, seeds and ribs removed, and finely chopped

3 tablespoons freshly squeezed lime juice

3 tablespoons olive oil

Salt and freshly ground black pepper to taste

2 (15-ounce) cans black beans, drained and rinsed

1 ripe papaya, peeled, seeded, and cut into ½-inch dice

½ medium jicama, peeled and cut into ½-inch dice

½ red bell pepper, seeds and ribs removed, cut into ½-inch dice

¼ cup chopped fresh cilantro

3 garlic cloves, peeled and minced

3 shallots, peeled and chopped

1 teaspoon ground cumin

¼ teaspoon ground cinnamon

⅓ cup freshly squeezed orange juice

3 tablespoons freshly squeezed lime juice

3 tablespoons sherry vinegar

Salt and cayenne to taste

⅓ cup olive oil

Black Bean and Papaya Salad

Yield: 6–8 servings | Active time: 20 minutes | Start to finish: 35 minutes

1. Combine beans, papaya, jicama, red pepper, and cilantro in a mixing bowl.

2. Combine garlic, shallots, cumin, cinnamon, orange juice, lime juice, vinegar, salt, and cayenne in a jar with a tight-fitting lid, and shake well. Add olive oil, and shake well again.

3. Toss salad with dressing, and refrigerate salad for at least 15 minutes before serving.

VARIATION: *Mango can be substituted for the papaya, and white beans can be used instead of black beans.*

Note: The salad can be made 1 day in advance and refrigerated, tightly covered.

---

1 pound dried pinto beans

2 bay leaves

1 tablespoon dried oregano

¼ pound bacon, cut into 1-inch segments

1 large onion, peeled and diced

1 large green bell pepper, seeds and ribs removed, and diced

3 garlic cloves, peeled and minced

2 tablespoons cider vinegar

Salt and freshly ground black pepper to taste

Stewed Beans

Yield: 6–8 servings | Active time: 20 minutes | Start to finish: 3 hours, including 1 hour for soaking

1. Place beans in a 4-quart saucepan and cover with cold water. Bring to a boil over high heat, covered, and boil for 1 minute. Remove the pan from the heat, and allow beans to soak for 1 hour, covered. (Alternately, soak beans in water to cover for a minimum of 6 hours or preferably overnight. With either method, cooking should progress as soon as beans are soaked.) Drain beans, and return them to the saucepan.

2. Cover beans with fresh water, add bay leaves and oregano, and bring to a boil over medium-high heat, stirring occasionally. Reduce the heat to low and simmer beans, covered, for 1 hour, or until beans are almost tender. Drain beans, reserving 2 cups of liquid. Remove and discard bay leaves. Return beans and reserved liquid to the saucepan.

3. While beans simmer, place bacon in a large skillet over medium-high heat. Cook until bacon is crisp, then remove bacon from the pan with a slotted spoon, and drain on paper towels. Discard all but 3 tablespoons of bacon fat.

4. Add onion, bell pepper, and garlic to the skillet and cook over medium-high heat, stirring frequently, for 3 minutes or until onion is translucent.

5. Add vegetables, vinegar, and bacon to beans, and stir well. Bring beans back to a boil, and simmer, uncovered, for 30 minutes or until very tender. Season to taste with salt and pepper, and serve hot.

Note: The beans can be prepared up to 2 days in advance and refrigerated, tightly covered. Reheat the beans over low heat, covered.

Potato Pudding

Yield: 6–8 servings | Active time: 20 minutes | Start to finish: 1½ hours

2 tablespoons vegetable oil

2 large onions, peeled and diced

Salt and freshly ground black pepper to taste

1 teaspoon granulated sugar

2 large eggs

6 tablespoons (¾ stick) unsalted butter, melted

2 tablespoons all-purpose flour

6 medium Idaho baking potatoes, peeled

1. Preheat the oven to 400°F, and grease a 9 x 13-inch baking dish.

2. Heat oil in a large skillet over medium-high heat. Add onions and cook, stirring frequently, for 3 minutes or until onions are translucent. Sprinkle onions with salt, pepper, and sugar. Increase the heat to high and cook onions, stirring frequently, until well browned. Set aside.

3. Combine eggs, melted butter, and flour in a mixing bowl, and whisk well. Grate potatoes, 1 at a time, in a food processor, using a shredding disk, or with a hand grater. Place each grated potato in a colander, and press with the back of a spoon to extract as much liquid as possible. Transfer potato to egg mixture and stir to coat; this prevents discoloration. Repeat with remaining potatoes, stir in onions, and season mixture with salt and pepper. Scrape mixture into prepared pan.

4. Bake pudding in the top third of the oven for 15 minutes, then reduce the temperature to 375°F and bake for an additional 45 minutes or until top is crisp and potatoes are tender. Cut into squares, and serve immediately.

Note: The pudding can be baked up to 2 days in advance and refrigerated, tightly covered. Reheat covered with aluminum foil in a 350°F oven for 15 minutes, then remove the foil and bake for an additional 10–15 minutes.

2 pounds small redskin potatoes, scrubbed

1 (1-pound) bag frozen peas and carrots

6 garlic cloves, peeled

2 egg yolks, at room temperature

¾ cup extra-virgin olive oil

1 tablespoon freshly squeezed lemon juice

Salt and freshly ground black pepper to taste

Garlicky Potato Salad

Yield: 6–8 servings | Active time: 15 minutes | Start to finish: 4 hours, including 3 hours to chill the potatoes

1. Place potatoes whole with skins in a large saucepan of cold salted water. Bring potatoes to a boil over high heat, reduce the heat to medium, and boil potatoes for 10–20 minutes, or until they are tender when pierced with the tip of a paring knife. Drain potatoes and chill well. Cut potatoes into ⅓-inch cubes and place them in a large mixing bowl.

2. Cook peas and carrots according to package directions, and add them to the bowl with potatoes to chill.

3. To prepare aioli sauce, combine garlic cloves and egg yolks in a food processor fitted with a steel blade or in a blender. Puree, then, with the machine running, very slowly add olive oil through the feed tube of the food processor or the top of the blender. When the sauce has emulsified and thickened, add lemon juice and season sauce to taste with salt and pepper.

4. Combine the sauce with salad, and serve chilled.

Note: The salad can be made 1 day in advance and refrigerated, tightly covered.

Garlicky Potato Salad

Garden Potato Salad

Yield: 6–8 servings | Active time: 20 minutes | Start to finish: 4 hours, including 3 hours to chill potatoes

2 pounds small redskin potatoes, scrubbed
1 cucumber, peeled
1 green bell pepper, seeds and ribs removed
1 small red onion, peeled
3 celery ribs, rinsed and trimmed
½ cup mayonnaise
3 tablespoons white wine vinegar
Salt and freshly ground black pepper to taste

1. Place potatoes in a large saucepan of cold salted water. Bring potatoes to a boil over high heat, reduce the heat to medium, and boil potatoes for 10–20 minutes, or until they are tender when pierced with the tip of a paring knife. Drain potatoes and chill well. Cut potatoes into 1-inch cubes, and place them in a large mixing bowl.

2. Cut cucumber in half lengthwise and scrape out the seeds with a teaspoon. Slice cucumber into thin arcs, and add to potatoes. Cut green pepper into 1-inch sections and slice each section into thin strips. Add to the mixing bowl. Cut onion in half through the root end, and cut each half into thirds. Cut into thin slices and add to the mixing bowl. Cut each celery rib in half lengthwise and thinly slice the celery. Add to the mixing bowl.

3. Toss potato salad with mayonnaise and vinegar, and season to taste with salt and pepper. Serve well chilled.

Note: The salad can be made 1 day in advance and refrigerated, tightly covered.

Tabbouleh with Feta

Yield: 6–8 servings | Active time: 20 minutes | Start to finish: 2 hours, including 1 hour for chilling

1 pound bulgur wheat
¾ cup freshly squeezed lemon juice
3 cups very hot water
1 cucumber, peeled, halved, seeded, and chopped
4 ripe plum tomatoes, rinsed, cored, seeded, and chopped
1 small red onion, peeled and chopped
2 garlic cloves, peeled and minced
1 cup chopped fresh parsley
3 tablespoons chopped fresh mint
1 cup crumbled feta cheese
½ cup olive oil
Salt and freshly ground black pepper to taste

1. Place bulgur in a large mixing bowl and add lemon juice and hot water. Let stand for 30 minutes, or until bulgur is tender. Drain off any excess liquid.

2. Add cucumbers, tomatoes, onion, garlic, parsley, mint, and feta to bulgur and toss to combine. Add olive oil a few tablespoons at a time to make salad moist but not runny. Season to taste with salt and pepper.

3. Refrigerate tabbouleh for at least 1 hour. Serve cold or at room temperature.

Tabbouleh with Feta

Chapter 16

Grilled Desserts

The title of this chapter is not an oxymoron, nor is it just variations on toasted marshmallows—although there is a recipe for S'mores leading it off. What you will find when cooking these recipes is that the grill is a natural way to glean the most luscious flavor from fruit; fruit desserts comprise the majority of these recipes. It should come as no surprise that heating enhances the fruits' natural sweetness, as well as creating a softer texture.

---

24 sweet whole-wheat crackers, such as Carr's wheatmeal biscuits

1½ (3-ounce) dark chocolate bars or any flavored chocolate bar, broken into ½-inch pieces

12 large marshmallows

Ultimately Messy S'mores

Yield: 4–6 servings | Active time: 10 minutes | Start to finish: 35 minutes

1. Prepare a medium-hot grill according to the instructions given in Chapter 1. Cut 12 (8-inch) squares of aluminum foil.

2. Place 1 cracker in the center of each foil sheet, and top with chocolate. Toast marshmallows over the grill on a long-handled fork, and place on top of chocolate. Top marshmallows with remaining crackers, and enclose sandwiches in foil.

3. Grill foil packets for 2 minutes, or until chocolate is melted and gooey. Unwrap, and serve immediately.

Ultimately Messy S'mores

Candy Bar Quesadillas

Yield: 4–6 servings | Active time: 10 minutes | Start to finish: 30 minutes

8 (8-inch) flour tortillas
Vegetable oil spray
1 (8-ounce) package cream cheese, softened
4 (2-ounce) candy bars, such as Snickers, Almond Joy, Milky Way, or any chocolate bar, each cut into 15 thin slices
4 tablespoons confectioners' sugar

1. Prepare a medium-hot grill according to the instructions given in Chapter 1.

2. Wrap tortillas in plastic wrap and microwave on high (100% power) for 20 seconds, or until pliable. Spray 4 tortillas with vegetable oil spray, and place them sprayed-side down on a cookie sheet. Spread each tortilla with ¼ of cream cheese to within ½ inch of the edge. Top cheese with candy bar slices.

3. Top with remaining 4 tortillas, and press with the palm of your hand or a spatula to close them firmly. Spray tops of quesadillas with vegetable oil spray.

4. Grill quesadillas, covered, for 2 minutes. Turn gently with a wide spatula and grill for an additional 2 minutes, or until brown and crisp. Remove quesadillas from the grill, and sprinkle with confectioners' sugar. Allow quesadillas to sit for 2 minutes, then cut each into 6 sections and serve immediately.

Note: The quesadillas can be prepared 1 day in advance of grilling them. Refrigerate them, tightly covered with plastic wrap, and bring them back to room temperature before grilling.

Toasted Cake with Berry Sauce

Yield: 4–6 servings | Active time: 15 minutes | Start to finish: 30 minutes

1 pint fresh strawberries, rinsed, stemmed, and sliced
½ pint fresh raspberries, rinsed
½ pint fresh blueberries, rinsed
2 tablespoons crème de cassis or Chambord
1 teaspoon grated lemon zest
4–6 (¾-inch) slices pound cake, homemade or purchased
1 pint strawberry ice cream, or your favorite flavor

1. Prepare a medium-hot grill according to the instructions given in Chapter 1.

2. Place ½ of strawberries in a food processor fitted with a steel blade or in a blender; puree until smooth. Combine puree, remaining strawberries, raspberries, blueberries, crème de cassis, and lemon zest in a mixing bowl, and stir well. Refrigerate, tightly covered, until ready to use.

3. Grill cake slices, uncovered if using a charcoal grill, for 1 minute per side or until grill marks appear. To serve, place cake slices on plates and top with ice cream and fruit sauce. Serve immediately.

Note: Fruit sauce can be made up to 1 day in advance and chilled, tightly covered.

4 Granny Smith apples, peeled, cored, and cut into ½-inch slices

2 tablespoons unsalted butter, melted

3 tablespoons granulated sugar

3 ounces sharp cheddar cheese

¼ cup honey, heated

Apples with Cheddar

Yield: 4–6 servings | Active time: 15 minutes | Start to finish: 35 minutes

1. Prepare a medium-hot grill according to the instructions given in Chapter 1.

2. Toss apple slices with butter, and sprinkle with sugar. Shave cheese into thin strips with a vegetable peeler, and set aside.

3. Grill apple slices for 3–4 minutes per side, covered, or until grill marks show and apples are tender. Remove apples from the grill with a spatula, and arrange on plates. Sprinkle cheese on top of apples, and drizzle honey over cheese and apples. Serve immediately.

4–6 navel oranges

1 pint fresh raspberries, rinsed

2 tablespoons granulated sugar

2 tablespoons Grand Marnier, triple sec, or another orange-flavored liqueur

1 pint vanilla ice cream or vanilla frozen yogurt

Grilled Oranges with Raspberry Sauce

Yield: 4–6 servings | Active time: 10 minutes | Start to finish: 30 minutes |

1. Prepare a medium-hot grill according to the instructions given in Chapter 1.

2. Grate 2 teaspoons zest off oranges, and then peel oranges. Cut each into 4 slices horizontally. Combine raspberries, sugar, Grand Marnier, and orange zest in a small mixing bowl. Mash fruit gently, and set aside.

3. Grill orange slices for 1½–2 minutes per side, uncovered if using a charcoal grill, or until browned. To serve, arrange orange slices on the bottom of bowls, and top with ice cream and raspberry sauce. Serve immediately.

Note: The raspberry sauce can be made up to 6 hours in advance and kept at room temperature.

Rum-Glazed Pineapple

Yield: 6–8 servings | Active time: 15 minutes | Start to finish: 30 minutes

1. Prepare a medium-hot grill according to the instructions given in Chapter 1.

2. Combine rum, butter, sugar, cinnamon, and vanilla in a small saucepan. Cook over medium heat, stirring frequently, for 15 minutes, or until thickened. Set aside.

3. While sauce simmers, cut rind off pineapple, and cut in half vertically. Cut out and discard core, and cut pineapple into ⅓-inch-thick slices. Set aside.

4. Grill pineapple slices for 1½–2 minutes per side, uncovered if using a charcoal grill, or until browned, brushing them with sauce frequently. To serve, cut pineapple slices into chunks, place on plates, and top with ice cream and additional sauce. Serve immediately, garnished with nuts, if using.

Note: The sauce can be made up to 2 days in advance and refrigerated, tightly covered. Reheat it over low heat or in a microwave oven before using.

¾ cup dark rum

8 tablespoons (1 stick) unsalted butter

¼ cup firmly-packed dark brown sugar

½ teaspoon ground cinnamon

¼ teaspoon pure vanilla extract

1 ripe pineapple

3–4 cups vanilla ice cream

½ cup chopped toasted walnuts (optional)

Rum-Glazed Pineapple

4–6 ripe peaches, unpeeled

¾ cup granulated sugar, divided

⅔ cup freshly squeezed orange juice

2 tablespoons freshly squeezed lemon juice, divided

¼ teaspoon pure vanilla extract

1 pint fresh raspberries, rinsed, or 1 (8-ounce) package frozen dry-packed raspberries, thawed

2 tablespoons Chambord or other berry-flavored liqueur

1 pint vanilla ice cream

Nouvelle Peach Melba

Yield: 4–6 servings | Active time: 20 minutes | Start to finish: 30 minutes

1. Prepare a medium-hot grill according to the instructions given in Chapter 1.

2. Cut peaches in half and discard stones. Place peaches in a 9 x 13-inch pan, cut-side up.

3. Combine ⅔ cup sugar, orange juice, 1 tablespoon lemon juice, and vanilla in a small saucepan, and stir well. Bring to a boil over medium-high heat, and boil for 2 minutes, stirring occasionally. Pour syrup over peaches, and set aside.

3. Combine raspberries, remaining sugar, remaining lemon juice, and Chambord in a food processor fitted with a steel blade or in a blender. Puree until smooth, and strain mixture. Refrigerate until ready to use.

4. Drain peaches, and grill skin-side up for 4 minutes, uncovered if using a charcoal grill, then turn peaches with tongs and grill skin-side down for an additional 3–4 minutes, or until peaches are tender. To serve, place 2 peach halves in the bottom of each bowl, and top with ice cream and raspberry sauce. Serve immediately.

Note: Raspberry sauce can be made up to 1 day in advance and refrigerated, tightly covered.

Nouvelle Peach Melba

Chapter 17

Other Sweet Endings

States such as Oregon and Washington are known for fruit trees, and you will find many recipes here that utilize this sweet cornucopia, along with such ingredients as pineapple and macadamia nuts from Hawaii. But desserts such as Strawberry Shortcake are national favorites, and my version of that tried and true American invention is here too.

Warm Ghirardelli Chocolate Tortes

1½ cups sweetened coconut flakes

1¼ cups all-purpose flour

1½ teaspoons baking powder

¼ teaspoon salt

4 large eggs

3 large egg yolks

1½ cups granulated sugar

1½ teaspoons pure vanilla extract, divided

1½ sticks unsalted butter, melted and cooled

½ cup well-stirred sweetened cream of coconut, such as Coco López

½ cup dark rum

1 (8-ounce) package cream cheese, softened

3 cups confectioners' sugar

1 teaspoon grated lemon zest

Coconut Rum Cake

Yield: 8 servings | Active time: 25 minutes | Star to finish: 4 hours, including 2 hours for cake to cool

1. Preheat the oven to 375°F, with the rack in middle. Lightly grease a 9-inch round layer pan, and line the bottom with a round of parchment paper. Lightly grease the parchment paper, and then flour the inside of the pan, tapping out excess flour over the sink or a garbage can.

2. Bake coconut flakes on a baking sheet for 5–7 minutes, or until browned. Remove coconut from the oven, and set aside. Reduce the oven temperature to 350°F.

3. Whisk together flour, baking powder, and salt in a small bowl. Whisk together eggs, egg yolks, sugar, and 1 teaspoon vanilla in a large bowl, beating until mixture is thick and lemon-colored. Add ½ cup toasted coconut, flour mixture, and butter, and whisk until just combined. Pour batter into the prepared pan, and rap the pan on the counter to expel air bubbles.

4. Bake cake for 45 minutes, or until golden brown and cake starts to pull away from the side of the pan. Cool in pan on a rack 10 minutes. Invert cake onto the rack and discard parchment. Cool 10 minutes more.

5. Combine cream of coconut and rum in a small bowl, and stir well. Remove 3 tablespoons of mixture, and set aside. Using a meat fork, poke holes in the bottom of cake, and brush coconut rum mixture on the bottom. Allow it to soak in, and repeat. Turn cake over on the rack, and slice off top so it is level. Spread remaining coconut rum mixture on top, and allow it to soak in. Allow cake to cool completely.

6. For icing, combine cream cheese, confectioners' sugar, remaining ½ teaspoon vanilla, lemon zest, and reserved coconut rum mixture in a food processor fitted with a steel blade. Process until smooth, and scrape into a bowl. Apply frosting to cake, and pat remaining 1 cup toasted coconut on the top.

Note: The cake can be baked and soaked with the coconut rum mixture up to 2 days in advance and kept at room temperature, tightly covered with plastic wrap. The cake can be frosted up to 1 day in advance and kept at room temperature, lightly covered.

Pineapple Upside-Down Cake

Yield: 8 servings | Active time: 25 minutes | Start to finish: 1¼ hours

1. Preheat the oven to 350°F.

2. Cut pineapple into ½-inch slices. Melt 6 tablespoons butter in a 10-inch oven-proof skillet over medium-high heat. Add brown sugar, and cook for 2 minutes, stirring constantly. Arrange pineapple over sugar, and place cherries in center, if using. Set aside.

3. Sift together flour, baking powder, cinnamon, and salt. Combine remaining 6 tablespoons butter and sugar in a mixing bowl and beat with an electric mixer at medium speed until light and fluffy. Beat in eggs, 1 at a time, beating well between each addition. Beat in 2 tablespoons rum and vanilla. Add half of flour mixture at low speed until just blended. Add pineapple juice and then second half of flour mixture. Spoon batter over pineapple in skillet.

4. Bake cake for 45 minutes, or until a knife inserted in the center comes out clean. Remove cake from the oven, and place it on a cooling rack for 5 minutes. Invert a plate over the skillet, and then invert cake onto the plate; replace any pineapple from the pan that stuck. Sprinkle remaining 2 tablespoons rum over top of cake. Serve warm or at room temperature.

Note: The cake can be made up to 1 day in advance and kept at room temperature, lightly covered. If you do not own an ovenproof skillet, cover the plastic handle of a skillet with a double layer of heavy duty aluminum foil to protect it from melting in the oven.

½ medium ripe pineapple, peeled, cored, and halved lengthwise

1½ sticks unsalted butter, softened, divided

¾ cup firmly packed light brown sugar

4–6 maraschino cherries, optional

1½ cups all-purpose flour

2 teaspoons baking powder

½ teaspoon ground cinnamon

¼ teaspoon salt

1 cup granulated sugar

2 large eggs

¼ cup dark rum, divided

1 teaspoon pure vanilla extract

1 tablespoon dark rum

½ cup unsweetened pineapple juice

Pineapple Upside-Down Cake

1 (9-inch) unbaked pie shell (homemade or purchased)

3 large eggs

½ cup granulated sugar

1 teaspoon pure vanilla extract

1¼ cups crème fraîche

1 pint fresh blueberries, rinsed

Blueberry Crème Fraîche Tart

Yield: 6–8 servings | Active time: 15 minutes | Start to finish: 2½ hours, including 2 hours for chilling

1. Preheat the oven to 375°F. Prick bottom and sides of pie crust with a fork, press in a sheet of parchment paper, and fill pie plate with dried beans, rice, or metal pie stones. Bake for 10–15 minutes. Remove weights and parchment, and bake an additional 15 minutes or until golden brown. Set aside, and reduce the oven temperature to 350°F.

2. While crust bakes, whisk eggs and sugar in the top of a double boiler for 2 minutes, or until thick and lemon colored. Add vanilla and crème fraîche, and stir well. Place mixture over simmering water in the bottom of the double boiler. Heat, stirring constantly, until the mixture is hot and starting to thicken.

3. Place blueberries in the bottom of pie shell and pour warm custard over them. Bake for 10 minutes or until custard is set. Chill for at least 2 hours before serving.

VARIATION: *Raspberries or blackberries can be substituted for the blueberries.*

Note: The pie can be baked 1 day in advance and refrigerated, tightly covered.

½ pound (2 sticks) unsalted butter, divided

3 cups all-purpose flour

⅓ cup granulated sugar

1 tablespoon cream of tartar

2¼ teaspoons baking soda

¼ teaspoon salt

2 cups heavy cream, divided

1 quart strawberries

⅓ cup crème de cassis or Chambord

⅓ cup confectioners' sugar

Strawberry Shortcake

Yield: 6 servings | Active time: 15 minutes | Start to finish: 40 minutes, including 10 minutes for cooling

1. Preheat the oven to 375°F and grease 2 baking sheets with 1 tablespoon butter. Combine flour, sugar, cream of tartar, baking soda, and salt in a medium mixing bowl. Melt 3 tablespoons butter, and set aside. Cut remaining butter into ¼-inch cubes.

2. Cut cubed butter into flour mixture using a pastry blender, 2 knives, or your fingertips until mixture resembles coarse meal. Add 1 cup cream, and blend until just blended.

3. Scrape dough onto a floured surface, and knead lightly. Roll dough to a thickness of ¾ inch. Cut out 6 (4-inch) rounds and place them on the baking sheet. Brush rounds with melted butter. Cut out 6 (2½-inch) rounds and place them on top of larger rounds. Brush tops with butter.

4. Bake for 15–17 minutes or until shortcakes are golden brown. Cool for at least 10 minutes on a wire rack.

5. While shortcakes bake, rinse strawberries, discard green caps , and slice. Toss strawberries with crème de cassis. Set aside. Just prior to serving, whip remaining 1 cup cream with confectioners' sugar until stiff peaks form.

6. To serve, mound strawberries on larger round, and top with whipped cream and smaller round. Serve immediately.

VARIATION: *Any berry can be substituted for the strawberries, as can peeled peach slices.*

Note: The shortcakes can be baked up to 6 hours in advance and kept at room temperature.

Strawberry Shortcake

2 cups macadamia nuts

3 large eggs

1 cup firmly packed light brown sugar

½ teaspoon pure vanilla extract

¼ teaspoon salt

4 tablespoons (½ stick) unsalted butter, melted

1 cup firmly packed sweetened, flaked coconut

1 pre-baked 9-inch pie shell

3–4 cups coconut ice cream (optional)

Macadamia Coconut Pie

Yield: 6–8 servings | Active time: 25 minutes | Start to finish: 2 hours, including 1 hour for cooling

1. Preheat the oven to 350°F. Bake macadamia nuts for 5–7 minutes, or until browned. Remove nuts from the oven and chop coarsely. Set aside.

2. Increase the oven temperature to 375˚F. Whisk eggs, brown sugar, vanilla, and salt until thick, and then whisk in butter. Stir in nuts and coconut, and scrape filling into pie shell.

3. Bake pie for 25–30 minutes, or until set in the center. Cool pie on a rack 1 hour, then serve, topped with ice cream, if using.

Note: The pie can be made up to 2 days in advance and kept at room temperature, lightly covered.

6 tablespoons (¾ stick) unsalted butter, divided

5 ounces bittersweet chocolate, chopped, divided

2 tablespoons heavy cream

1 tablespoon rum or fruit-flavored liqueur

2 large eggs

1 large egg yolk

¼ cup granulated sugar

¼ cup all-purpose flour

Sweetened whipped cream or ice cream (optional)

Warm Ghirardelli Chocolate Tortes

Yield: 6 servings | Active time: 20 minutes | Start to finish: 35 minutes

1. Grease 6 muffin cups with 1 tablespoon butter. Melt 2 ounces chocolate with cream and rum in a small microwave-safe dish. Stir well and refrigerate to harden. Form chocolate into 6 balls and refrigerate until ready to use.

2. Preheat the oven to 350°F. Melt remaining chocolate with remaining butter and allow to cool.

3. Combine eggs, egg yolk, and sugar in a medium mixing bowl. Beat with an electric mixer at medium and then high speed until very thick and triple in volume. Fold cooled chocolate into eggs, and then fold in flour.

4. Divide batter among the muffin cups and push a chocolate ball into the center of each cup. Bake tortes for 10–12 minutes, or until sides are set. Remove the muffin pan from the oven and invert tortes onto a baking sheet. Move tortes to individual serving plates, and serve immediately, with whipped cream or ice cream, if using.

Note: The tortes can be prepared up to 2 hours before baking them.

Lemon Squares

Yield: 12 pieces | Active time: 15 minutes | Start to finish: 1 hour

1. Preheat the oven to 350°F.

2. Combine butter, confectioners' sugar, 1 cup flour, and salt in a mixing bowl and mix thoroughly with a wooden spoon. Press mixture into an 8-inch square pan. Bake for 20 minutes, or until set and lightly brown. Remove crust from the oven, and set aside.

3. While crust is baking, combine eggs, granulated sugar, remaining 2 tablespoons flour, lemon juice, and lemon zest in a mixing bowl. Beat with an electric mixer on medium speed for 1 minute, or until well blended. Pour topping over crust and bake for 20 minutes, or until barely brown. The custard should still be soft. Cool the pan on a cooling rack, then cut into 12 pieces and dust with confectioners' sugar, if desired.

Note: The lemon squares can be refrigerated for up to 1 week, tightly covered with plastic wrap.

½ cup (1 stick) unsalted butter, melted

¼ cup confectioners' sugar

1 cup plus 2 tablespoons all-purpose flour

Pinch of salt

2 large eggs, at room temperature

1 cup granulated sugar

⅓ cup freshly squeezed lemon juice

2 teaspoons grated lemon zest

Lemon Squares

1 cup chopped hazelnuts

¼ pound (1 stick) unsalted
   butter, softened

1⅓ cups firmly packed light
   brown sugar

2 large eggs, at room
   temperature

1 teaspoon pure vanilla
   extract

1 cup all-purpose flour

Pinch of salt

1 cup white chocolate
   pieces

White Chocolate Hazelnut Brownies

Yield: 12 pieces | Active time: 15 minutes | Start to finish: 1½ hours, including 30 minutes for cooling

1. Bake hazelnuts for 5–7 minutes, or until browned. Remove nuts from the oven, and set aside.

2. Preheat the oven to 350°F, and grease an 8-inch square pan.

3. Combine butter and brown sugar in a mixing bowl and beat with an electric mixer on low speed to combine. Raise the speed to high and beat for 2 minutes, or until light and fluffy. Reduce the mixer speed to medium and beat in eggs, one at a time, and vanilla. Reduce the speed to low and add flour and salt. Mix until just blended. Stir in hazelnuts and white chocolate pieces, and spread batter in an even layer in the prepared pan.

4. Bake for 40 minutes, or until a toothpick inserted in the center comes out clean. Cool brownies on a cooling rack for at least 30 minutes, then cut them into 12 pieces.

Note: The brownies can be made up to 3 days in advance and kept at room temperature, tightly covered with plastic wrap.

Appendix A
Metric Conversion Tables

The scientifically precise calculations needed for baking are not necessary when cooking conventionally. The tables in this appendix are designed for general cooking. If making conversions for baking, grab your calculator and compute the exact figure.

Converting Ounces to Grams

The numbers in the following table are approximate. To reach the exact amount of grams, multiply the number of ounces by 28.35.

OUNCES	GRAMS
1 ounce	30 grams
2 ounces	60 grams
3 ounces	85 grams
4 ounces	115 grams
5 ounces	140 grams
6 ounces	180 grams
7 ounces	200 grams
8 ounces	225 grams
9 ounces	250 grams
10 ounces	285 grams
11 ounces	300 grams
12 ounces	340 grams
13 ounces	370 grams
14 ounces	400 grams
15 ounces	425 grams
16 ounces	450 grams

Converting Quarts to Liters

The numbers in the following table are approximate. To reach the exact amount of liters, multiply the number of quarts by 0.95.

QUARTS	LITERS
1 cup (¼ quart)	¼ liter
1 pint (½ quart)	½ liter
1 quart	1 liter
2 quarts	2 liters
2½ quarts	2½ liters
3 quarts	2¾ liters
4 quarts	3¾ liters
5 quarts	4¾ liters
6 quarts	5½ liters
7 quarts	6½ liters
8 quarts	7½ liters

Converting Pounds to Grams and Kilograms

The numbers in the following table are approximate. To reach the exact amount of grams, multiply the number of pounds by 453.6.

POUNDS	GRAMS; KILOGRAMS
1 pound	450 grams
1½ pounds	675 grams
2 pounds	900 grams
2½ pounds	1,125 grams; 1¼ kilograms
3 pounds	1,350 grams
3½ pounds	1,500 grams; 1½ kilograms
4 pounds	1,800 grams
4½ pounds	2 kilograms
5 pounds	2¼ kilograms
5½ pounds	2½ kilograms
6 pounds	2¾ kilograms
6½ pounds	3 kilograms
7 pounds	3¼ kilograms
7½ pounds	3½ kilograms
8 pounds	3¾ kilograms

Converting Fahrenheit to Celsius

The numbers in the following table are approximate. To reach the exact temperature, subtract 32 from the Fahrenheit reading, multiply the number by 5, and then divide by 9.

DEGREES FAHRENHEIT	DEGREES CELSIUS
170°F	77°C
180°F	82°C
190°F	88°C
200°F	95°C
225°F	110°C
250°F	120°C
300°F	150°C
325°F	165°C
350°F	180°C
375°F	190°C
400°F	205°C
425°F	220°C
450°F	230°C
475°F	245°C
500°F	260°C

Converting Inches to Centimeters

The numbers in the following table are approximate. To reach the exact number of centimeters, multiply the number of inches by 2.54.

INCHES	CENTIMETERS
½ inch	1.5 centimeters
1 inch	2.5 centimeters
2 inches	5 centimeters
3 inches	8 centimeters
4 inches	10 centimeters
5 inches	13 centimeters
6 inches	15 centimeters
7 inches	18 centimeters
8 inches	20 centimeters
9 inches	23 centimeters
10 inches	25 centimeters
11 inches	28 centimeters
12 inches	30 centimeters

Appendix B

Measurement Tables

Table of Weights and Measures of Common Ingredients		
FOOD	QUANTITY	YIELD
Apples	1 pound	2½ to 3 cups sliced
Avocado	1 pound	1 cup mashed fruit
Bananas	1 medium	1 cup, sliced
Bell Peppers	1 pound	3 to 4 cups sliced
Blueberries	1 pound	3⅓ cups
Butter	¼ pound (1 stick)	8 tablespoons
Cabbage	1 pound	4 cups packed shredded
Carrots	1 pound	3 cups diced or sliced
Chocolate, morsels	12 ounces	2 cups
Chocolate, bulk	1 ounce	3 Tablespoons. grated
Cocoa powder	1 ounce	¼ cup
Coconut, flaked	7 ounces	2½ cups
Cream	½ pint = 1 cup	2 cups whipped
Cream cheese	8 ounces	1 cup
Flour	1 pound	4 cups
Lemons	1 medium	3 tablespoons juice
Lemons	1 medium	2 teaspoons zest
Milk	1 quart	4 cups
Molasses	12 ounces	1½ cups
Mushrooms	1 pound	5 cups sliced
Onions	1 medium	½ cup chopped
Peaches	1 pound	2 cups sliced
Peanuts	5 ounces	1 cup
Pecans	6 ounces	1½ cups
Pineapple	1 medium	3 cups diced fruit

Potatoes	1 pound	3 cups sliced
Raisins	1 pound	3 cups
Rice	1 pound	2–2½ cups raw
Spinach	1 pound	¾ cup cooked
Squash, summer	1 pound	3½ cups sliced
Strawberries	1 pint	1½ cups sliced
Sugar, brown	1 pound	2¼ cups, packed
Sugar, confectioners'	l pound	4 cups
Sugar, granulated	1 pound	2¼ cups
Tomatoes	1 pound	1½ cups pulp
Walnuts	4 ounces	1 cup

Table of Liquid Measurements	
Pinch	Less than ⅛ teaspoon
3 teaspoons	1 tablespoon
2 tablespoons	1 fluid ounce
8 tablespoons	½ cup
2 cups	1 pint
1 quart	2 pints
1 gallon	4 quarts

Index